# Praise for Leadership Simplified

"This book is a 'must read' for anyone who wishes to be the best they can be in the business world. Doug Van Dyke's communication methods and techniques will not only help leaders improve or polish up their business skills, but will also help them build a better team environment with improved upstream and downstream communication all around. There are also valuable techniques I had never seen before that make a lot of sense to use. Definitely a winning methodology."

Lee Peterson, Serial Entrepreneur

"If you want to communicate more effectively, increase team collaboration, make meaningful presentations, or simply run meetings better, read this book! Leadership Simplified has helped me to be a better leader, and in the process, helped my team achieve more."

Mark Linsky, Regional Sales Manager
Assurant Employee Benefits Corporation

"Using the valuable information and communication strategies contained in this book has had an immediate and positive influence on my personal and business relationships."

Joel Van Citters, President
All Media Productions

"Leadership Simplified is the real deal – if you have to interact with people in a business environment, you must read this book. You will love the clear and concise manner in which it is laid out – fully supported by meaningful, real-life situations. Doug Van Dyke's book has found a permanent spot on my desk, as my 'Survival Guide!'"

Bill Lee, Human Resources Manager
SYSCO Foods, West Coast Florida

"Doug Van Dyke has linked two important topics: leadership and the effectiveness needed to lead. Leadership Simplified is a great and easy read, chock full of clear examples and analogies laced with practical guidance. Doug correctly covers leadership as the development of vision with the ability to assert that vision through the art of persuasion and team building. Probably more importantly, he links vision with effectiveness which requires the discipline to do many small, but critical, things consistently right in terms of ethics and communication skills. The book is a must read if you want to kick it up a few levels and actually lead."

Jerry Custin, Colonel (retired), United States Air Force
President/CEO
Upper Tampa Bay Chamber of Commerce

"Leadership Simplified contains clear, practical, and easy to implement pointers that can dramatically improve the performance of any leader with little effort. Don't read it and put in on a shelf. Lay it on your desk. When you first glance at your calendar for the day, look at your tasks for that day. Whether the tasks are giving a presentation, holding a meeting, interviewing a candidate, whatever they are, just quickly scan the sections of the book that apply to reload in your mind the key success factors for those activities. Do that for a few weeks and you will double your effectiveness."

Howard Baskin, Advisory Board Chairman
Big Cat Rescue

"A fast-paced, enjoyable read packed with useful items for all levels of leaders."

Gisell Galan, Business Development Manager
Gevity, Inc.

"Finally, a book about leadership in plain English. Leadership Simplified is easy to read, logical, and succinct. One of my favorite parts is the "Bottom Line" that summarizes the major takeaways of each chapter. This is definitely a reference book for anybody who believes in self-improvement."

Irene Hurst, Director, MBA Programs
College of Business
University of South Florida

# Leadership Simplified

## The Field Guide for the Savvy Leader

Doug Van Dyke, MBA

Global Market Publishing

Copyright © DVD Consulting Incorporated, 2009
All Rights Reserved.

Published by Global Market Publishing

Unless otherwise stated or footnoted all names and characters referenced in this book are the product of the author's imagination or are used fictitiously, and any resemblance to actual persons, living or dead, is entirely coincidental.

No part of this publication may be reproduced, stored in a retrieval system or transmitted in any way by any means, electronic, mechanical, photocopy, recording or otherwise, without the prior written permission of DVD Consulting Incorporated, except as provided by USA copyright law.

ISBN: 978-0-9819202-0-7

Cover Design by DVD Consulting Incorporated
Printed in the United States

For Veronica
My partner in business, my partner in love, my partner in life.

# Contents

# Acknowledgements

UNDERTAKING the creation of a book is not for the meek. It is also not for lone wolves. As such, I am honored to have been supported by so many talented and interested people. **My heartfelt thanks** to all of the following: to Veronica Van Dyke and Joan Eldridge for their seemingly ever flowing red pens. The Lee's: Bill Lee and Lee Peterson for their fantastic feedback and ideas. Joel Van Citters and Howard Baskin for their incredible insight and marvelous attention to detail. And to Jerry Custin, Randy Hafer, David Miller, Cindy Krueger, and Ken Schmidt for your input and enhancements.

I would be remiss if I did not acknowledge my parents, Doris and Ron, for the love and guidance they have bestowed upon me all these years. The principles and lessons you have taught me serve as the bedrock for this narrative. Thank you and I love you.

# Preface

"The most difficult thing is the decision to act, the rest is merely tenacity. The fears are paper tigers. You can do anything you decide to do. You can act to change and control your life; and the procedure, the process is its own reward."

—Amelia Earhart, American aviator, 1897 – 1937

THIS book is about action: results, growing skills, enhancing technique, getting things done. Also, this book is between you and me. I want to talk with you and share facts, ideas, and concepts. In addition, I have sought to structure each chapter so as to get to the heart of the matter as quickly as possible. Hopefully this book will resonate with you and stir action. Who knows, while reading it you may even smile a time or two.

Feel free to skip around. Review the Table of Contents and flip to a topic that interests you. Successful people are busy, so do not hesitate to go directly to a section that will help you quickly embrace a fresh idea or pick up a new business tool. In short, use this book however it will enhance your effectiveness.

My experience over the past twenty-five years is that people who take action are successful. Mind you, action does not always lead to success. It is merely an attempt to move forward, and forward-thinkers drive accomplishment and innovation. In any case, it is my hope that you use this book as a field guide. It is packed full of proven items developed while coaching thousands of professionals and working with hundreds of organizations throughout the United States.

Now let's get started!

# Chapter 1

# Leadership Reinvention

IN the 1980's Chuck Daly was tapped on the shoulder to coach the Detroit Pistons. He did fairly well and led the team into the NBA playoffs. In fact, they became the highest scoring team in the league. Year after year, however, they got spanked (that's a basketball term for not winning) in the playoffs. While still successful by many measures, the team was seemingly underachieving. Chuck Daly grew frustrated and sought to lead his team to a higher level of success. What did he do? He analyzed his team's situation and potential. In addition, he analyzed the competition and various trends in the league. Finally, he came to two conclusions: 1. Defense wins championships. 2. He needed to transform the Pistons into the best defensive team in the league. And so Chuck Daly ceased being satisfied with just reaching the playoffs and set his sights on winning an NBA championship.

When he approached his team about becoming the best defensive team in the league, the players laughed. They all thought he was joking. Their smiles dissipated however, as Chuck's unwavering, steely stare informed them that he was dead serious. Ultimately, a consensus was reached and the team decided that they would do whatever it took to become the best defensive team in the league.

It took hard work and dedication – those of you who are basketball players know that it takes more energy to play defense than offense. Also, it is a lot less fun. Soon the Pistons were nowhere near the top of the league in offense. But, they had become the best defensive team in the game.

What happened to Chuck Daly's Detroit Pistons? Well, by 1989 they became world champions. In fact, they became back-to-back champions. So what can we learn today that Chuck and his team discovered in the 1980's? Something exciting really – powerful reinventions can occur with the same leader and the same team! That's right, the Pistons experienced a dramatic transformation with predominately the same people, and found heightened success.

Just how the heck did big Chuck and the "Bad Boy" Pistons do it? They followed five core principles:

1. They pragmatically analyzed their current situation and created an attainable vision.
2. They communicated effectively.
3. A consensus was reached that created buy-in, commitment, and a sense of excitement.
4. Measures, metrics, and dashboards were crafted in order to track and rank progress.
5. Excellent execution, targeted coaching, and unabashed celebration took place along the way.

Let's step back for a moment and look at Chuck Daly. He totally reinvented himself in order to lead his team where they needed to go. In other words, he decided that the team did not need a new leader or new players. He decided that the team needed a new direction and perspective. And he was confident that he possessed the kind of vision and skills that were necessary to lead his team to the Promised Land.

It has been my observation that leaders frequently become comfortable and set in their ways with regard to certain leadership styles, techniques, and language. Heck, it makes logical sense. When you hone habits and actions that catapult you to success why not stick with them? By relying on the same winning formula year after year, however, leaders can sometimes become stale or passé. Insightful leaders seek to remain agile. After all, their workforce is constantly changing, their pace of business is quickening, and globalization is altering their competitive and opportunistic landscape. The best leaders engage in continual reinvention as they enhance their winning formula to best fit in a changing world. Reinvention offers an opportunity to remain relevant and effective.

Consider this: in the twentieth century Penn Central Railroad (once a fine company) failed. Why did Penn Central fail? Answer: their leaders thought they were in the railroad industry – so that was the only marketplace in which they competed. In reality, they were part of the transportation industry. As such, they should have developed competitive product lines for automobiles, trucks, airlines, and shipping. They did not reinvent even though they had ample opportunity and resources to do so. The result: when the marketplace changed and competition heated up, Penn Central went out of business. Our job in the 21st century is to not fall into the same complacency trap.

Insightful leaders seek to remain agile. After all, their workforce is constantly changing, their pace of business is quickening, and globalization is altering their competitive and opportunistic landscape.

How do we avoid Penn Central's fate? As leaders we can propel our success and lead our teams to greater heights by embracing a five-part approach.

Part I: Analysis, Agility, and Visioning
Part II: Communication
Part III: Setting the Course and Creating Buy-In
Part IV: Measures, Metrics, and Structure
Part V: Execution, Coaching, and Celebration

The remainder of this book delves into tools and techniques that will assist you with this straight-forward process. Keep in mind: you are already good or else you would not be in a leadership position. As such, everything contained in this book is not an absolute. Pick and choose items that resonate with you and strategically fit with your skill base and situation.

So now we bid adieu to Penn Central, as well as Big Chuck and his Pistons. After all, this book is not about railroads or basketball. Rather, it is about you, your team, and how everyone can win big!

## Bottom Line

We must deepen and broaden our skills in order to continually elevate overall performance in our turbulent work world. For life-long learners, who desire to grow, it is an exciting prospect filled with limitless opportunity.

# PART I

# Analysis, Agility, and Visioning

*Analysis is the process of self-examination, coupled with sound evaluation of your team, competition, and industry. When performed objectively, analysis can reveal refreshing opportunities that lead to inspired visioning. The visioning process fleshes out the possible. Viable paths then emerge that can lead to enhanced success. It is not critical that the best path is chosen, only a good path. What ultimately matters is effective implementation.*

## CHAPTER 2

# Agility – Obliterating Analysis Paralysis

"....others plod and plod; however it is the agile that are able to leapfrog over the purely methodical and reach for the ring first."

—Anonymous

MANY PEOPLE get caught up in analysis. They slice and dice information in so many ways that they eventually become confused and overwhelmed – stuck in a sticky web of information overload. This typically results in procrastination or delays in creating strategies. Productivity and positive results suffer in the process.

Rather than analysis, think agility. According to Webster's, Agile is defined as: "Being mentally quick and resourceful; marked by the ready ability to move with quick ease and grace." Being agile equates to being proactive – thinking and changing on the fly – being agile is a critical quality for leaders and teams to possess in the twenty-first century business world. Just how do leaders demonstrate and teach agility? They keep it simple and ask great questions. Consider the following seven actions:

mirror. Perform periodic self-assessments. available resources such as personality and More importantly, ask yourself six pointed

- I adjusted my leadership style in the past?
- What were the positive results?
- What would I have done differently?
- Which skills sets are ripe for adjustment now?
- What are my three biggest strengths as a leader?
- What are three strengths that I admire in other leaders?

2. **Examine the marketplace**. Leaders are often so busy with their own initiatives that they run with their heads down. Take a breath, look up, and survey the competitive landscape. This can easily and quickly be accomplished by reviewing market reports, talking with "friendly" competitors, and honestly answering the following questions:

- Are my fingers on the pulse of the marketplace?
- What changes in the past year, five years, and ten years have shaped my marketplace?
- Did I anticipate past major changes or was I surprised by them?
- Who are three people I know that clearly understand the marketplace today? Do I trust them?
- What are three reliable sources of statistical and demographic information regarding my marketplace?
- What current trends will shape the future of my marketplace?

3. **Connect with strategic allies**. A strategic ally can be a co-worker, a vendor, a professor, a friend, or a loved one. However you define it, seek candid feedback from people who have insight, acumen, and who value your success. Ask them to:

- Assess you and your skills
- Predict future marketplace trends
- Share feedback regarding your team
- Share their intuition regarding the winds of business change
- Identify specific areas in which to grow stronger

4. **Make the customer king**. Without customers any business is sunk. So why are many leaders so squeamish about asking for customer feedback? Typically, customers are glad to share feedback with leaders. In addition, customer feedback often contains gold that can only be mined from their perspective. Consider tapping into the mind of your customer through any or all of the following means:

- Surveys: these can be created internally or purchased from industry specialists. They are a quick, easy, inexpensive method to gather feedback. If you choose to create a customer survey, seek to ask ten questions or less and make certain to include a section for additional comments.

- One-on-one interviews: certainly the most personal method to receive customer feedback. The key to maximizing this type of feedback is to ensure that the customer is comfortable. As such, consider holding the interview at their office, or a place they recommend.

- Roundtables: these are my personal favorite. Seek to gather five to seven similar type customers (i.e., best customers, new customers, well-tenured customers, etc.) A cross-section of types often creates confusion and digressive conversation. Always seek to have an odd number so that if opinions differ a majority can be established. While there is nothing wrong with the leader facilitating the discussion (facilitative leadership is discussed in the second part of this book), it is usually more beneficial to have an outside professional lead the group. This affords the leader the opportunity to better concentrate on the conversation, observe behavior, and remain impartial.

Once customer feedback has been gathered, ask yourself these questions:

- How do the results compare with the last customer survey, interview, or roundtable?
- What seems to have improved?
- Are any perceptions worse?
- Do customers seem receptive to new products, services, or processes?

5. **Review internal performance data and reports**. It is wise to take some time and review the internal performance records that have been created. The key to this action is to set a time limit for reviewing internal data. Make a commitment to yourself or your leadership team to complete your evaluation within a stated number of hours or days. Then stick to your commitment. Getting stuck in analysis paralysis will undermine the effectiveness of the review process.

set a time limit for reviewing internal data.

6. **Review the troops**. After you have assessed the marketplace, received customer feedback, and examined performance data, it is time to take a pragmatic look at your team. Ask yourself some tough questions:

- How has my team attempted to improve in the past?
- What were our biggest successes as a result?
- What should we have done differently?
- Are the right staff members on board? If not, list the positions, job duties, or individual(s) that should be included.
- What staff members are not a good fit? This is a particularly tough question. No one likes firing, demoting or reassigning team members. However, the failure to do so when the time is right is nothing short of neglectful. At a minimum, a strong development plan should be created for underperformers. Many times, however, the correct solution is the creation of an exit plan and bidding them adieu.
- Is every team member positioned so that they are doing tasks that showcase their strengths? Studies have shown that matching job tasks with the strengths of staff members leads to a 25% or better impact on performance.[1]

7. **Tap into your team**. Now is the time to ask your team targeted questions that will unlock important information for you to consider. Since most leaders work with teams that possess a variety of different personalities, it makes sense that leaders would use different management styles for different staff members. The following questions are a guide to assist leaders and managers in determining how their staff members like to be led. The answers revealed are often the difference between boosting team productivity and engaging in the unproductive process of termination.

- How do you like to be managed? (i.e., autonomously, highly structured environment, etc.)
- How do you like to be praised? (i.e., publicly, privately, verbally, in writing)

- How do you like to be rewarded? (i.e., prizes, time off, money)
- What moves you? This is one of the most critical pieces of information a leader can know. You may think that someone is motivated by money, but usually their passion lies elsewhere. It may be music, or sports, or chocolate, or travel. It is your job to know, and to lead and motivate accordingly.
- What level of directness do you prefer during conversations or when receiving feedback?
- What is expected of you at work? The key here is for you to understand, in their terms, what team members believe is expected of them. On occasion, there is disconnection between a team member's answer and what is in your mind.
- Do you feel a strong sense of purpose when you arrive at work? Why or why not?

## Bottom Line

Regular analysis of the marketplace, the competition, yourself, and your team is good business. It should also be conducted expeditiously with a set time limit for completion. If you seek to maintain an empowered, proactive workforce, consider introducing the concept of agility into your corporate culture.

# Chapter 3

# I Can See Clearly Now

JOHNNY Nash said it best when he sang: "I can see clearly now, the rain is gone." The rain in this instance is items that distort our vision, skewing what is possible. Too many times we constrain ourselves by allowing perceived hurdles to alter our focus. Likewise, difficult or challenging goals are sometimes a tough sell to a complacent team. However, by embracing a visioning system that opens our eyes to great possibilities, leaders can craft a focusable path. The ability to craft, effectively communicate, and implement a strategic vision is what defines a true leader – and separates them from a manager. The visioning process is segmented as follows:

> By embracing a visioning system that opens our eyes to great possibilities, leaders can craft a focusable path.

- Selecting the proper setting for a visioning session
- Brainstorming
- Crafting the vision

## Setting for Visioning

Let's face it, most boardrooms are not overly creative places. Yet, visioning is a creative process. As such, it deserves a fresh setting and creative materials. Take your team offsite to a place where they cannot check their email during each break. Your choices range from offsite meeting rooms to ropes courses to paintball. As you tap into your team, find out what offsite setting resonates with them and then go there. Remember, the location of the offsite does not have to be exotic – a hotel meeting room where you have not been before typically does just fine.

## Brainstorming

"Let's brainstorm on that!" How often have you heard or said those words? Brainstorming is a topic that is brought up with some regularity, yet so few leaders really know the proper rules of brainstorming. Rules? Yes, there are rules for darn near everything in this crazy, fast-paced world and brainstorming is no exception. There are eight simple, yet important rules, and here they are:

1. **Define the parameters**. In other words, make certain that the purpose or subject matter of the brainstorming session is clear in the minds of the participants.

2. **Treat every idea like a great idea**. The concept here is not to discourage anyone from participating. Thus, even though Bob from Marketing has suggested yet another hare-brained scheme, seek to remain calm. Respect Bob's input and use your facilitation skills to elicit the thoughts of other, more lucid members of the group. If the group scoffs at anyone's idea, protect the idea giver, while still encouraging everyone to participate.

3. **Keep your opinions on the sidelines**. Many a brainstorming session gets derailed because the person leading the group shares their own opinions and ideas, thus negatively altering the creative flow of the session. The communication section of this book contains a piece on facilitative leadership that may be of great assistance to the leader who opts to lead their own brainstorming session in lieu of engaging an outside facilitator. No matter who leads the brainstorming session, it is important that they remain a neutral part of the process.

4. **Do not go immediately into solution mode**. Invariably, someone is going to offer a terrific idea that will energize the group. What tends to happen next is that the leader allows the group to run with that idea. This action ordains the idea a "winner" and crushes subsequent creative thought. The challenge here is not to let the group get ahead of themselves. Praise the idea giver and the group. Also, let them know that there will be plenty of time later in the session to brainstorm on details surrounding the best ideas. Then refocus the group and make certain that all topical ideas are fleshed out prior to moving to the "drill down" phase.

5. **Encouragement**. Keep the hands rising and the ideas flowing by being positive. Encourage your team via language such as, "these ideas are great, who else has a comment or an idea?" Avoid calling on people and putting them on the spot. Let the participation and the ideas flow naturally.

6. **Voting**. Once you are certain that all ideas have been unveiled, seek your team's opinion on what ideas they most embrace. Their feedback can reveal if they value the priorities that are important to you. Some voting techniques to consider include the following:

- Secret ballot. This is best when sensitive material is involved or you are concerned about peer pressure biasing the voting.
- Raised hands. This quick and casual approach keeps the pace of the session moving along without the disruption of balloting.
- Voting groups. Divide the participants into smaller groups of three to four people. Each group reaches a consensus and then each group tenders one vote.

7. **Flesh it out**. After the top brainstorming idea(s) have been selected, take the team through them one-by-one. Drill down on details that support each identified idea. If additional key ideas are suggested, jot them down but do not digress into them. Rather, keep the group focused on the handful of ideas they voted on and tap into their mounting creative juices.

8. **Summarize**. The reason most brainstorming sessions fall flat is the leader's failure to distribute a summary of what was shared – and what follow up actions occurred. Without feedback, recognition, and guidance, how can we expect people to get excited about sharing their precious ideas with us? As such, at the end of the brainstorming session share a verbal summary with them. In addition, commit to a timeframe in which they can expect to receive a written summary of the session's findings. Then, deliver the summary on time and follow up appropriately on the actions that were highlighted.

If led correctly, the process of brainstorming yields an abundance of insights and ideas. At a minimum, it is a terrific teambuilding experience, as well as an opportunity to applaud your team for their creative ideas.

## Visioning

With the brainstorming process properly completed, it is now imperative to keep your team thinking creatively during visioning. Do your best to inject a unique ingredient into the session in order to spur creative thought. My experience has shown that Play Doh fits the bill nicely (more about that in a moment).

Once settled in to your offsite location, challenge your team with an activity. Break them into groups of four or five people and ask them this question: "What will our team look like in one year and what are the key qualities and achievements that will drive our success during the journey?" As the groups ponder this question, pass out Play Doh or some other materials and request that they make a physical representation that answers the question. In my opinion, the jewel of this exercise is the priceless expression on people's faces after the exercise has been explained and you pass out Play Doh. Once they delve into the exercise, however, I guarantee you that they will laugh, have fun, and collaboratively create a meaningful, attainable vision for your consideration.

The core deliverable of a visioning exercise is to have your team drill down on specific actions and results that will make their vision a reality.

The core deliverable of a visioning exercise is to have your team drill down on specific actions and results that will make their vision a reality. Far too many visioning sessions seem profound, but merely result in vague statements that fail to ignite spirit or encourage action. Don't fall into that trap. Engage your people. Place them in a creative, fun setting and challenge them to bring to life understandable and meaningful actions.

By the end of the brainstorming session and visioning process you will have a bevy of information that can be formalized into appropriate direction and strategies. The next part of this book contains an abundance of tools and techniques that will help you enhance your communication style in a powerful way.

## Bottom Line

By placing your team in a unique setting and leading them through a brainstorming process, you elevate the possibility of creating a future vision that will be meaningful, executable, and embraced by your team.

# Part II

# Communication

*Effective communication is critical to professional and personal success. It is also a crucial element in propelling individual or group skills to a higher level. Yet, communicating in the same manner as in the past does not aid in raising the bar. By honing and enhancing the manner in which we communicate, we can create a sense of excitement that will signal powerful change that leads to immediate results.*

## Chapter 4

# The Art of Moving Groups

IT may seem odd to start off this section with the advanced topic of presentation skills. Perhaps you were expecting non-verbal communication or something of that nature. Well, the reason I am starting with presentation skills is that successful leaders possess the ability to positively impact groups of people. With the advent of videoconferencing, YouTube and the like, it is almost a requirement for leaders to appear comfortable and natural in a public speaking setting. In addition, by enhancing the important skill of group presentation you will, more than likely, take your one-on-one communication skills to an even higher level. This section begins with a question:

> successful leaders possess the ability to positively impact groups of people.

> Have you ever been in the audience during a presentation that was so boring you thought you would lose your will to live?

We all have, and it's painful. Unfortunately, a majority of speakers in the business world are less than stellar. But it does not have to be that way. While many speakers have natural acumen, most great speakers are made, not born. Armed with powerful tools and a positive mindset, public presentations can be turned into something fun and meaningful. So let's take a look at some fundamentals that can make anyone an engaging speaker.

This chapter is divided into five, crisp segments:

- Success Factors
- Preparation
- Techniques
- Structures
- Post-presentation Actions

## Segment 1: Success Factors

When faced with the task of public speaking does your face appear as though you suddenly ingested a lemon? If so, you are not alone. Statistically, speaking in public is our greatest fear – even more so than snakes, going to the dentist, and death! Based on my experience, as well as discussions with hundreds of speaking professionals, there are five core ingredients to reducing your fears and delivering a successful presentation.

1. Practice, Practice, Practice

The most important ingredient is to practice! When I say practice what I mean is to rehearse the presentation, out loud, in a setting similar to the one in which you will be speaking. Also, practice your presentation <u>at least</u> three to five times prior to making the presentation. In other words, if you are giving a fifteen minute presentation and you want to be successful, practice a minimum of 45 minutes. While practicing, inject humor and side comments – just like you will during the real presentation.

The most important ingredient is to practice!

It is important to take note of what practice <u>is not</u>. For instance, silently reading your presentation is NOT practice. Saying your presentation aloud in the car while you are driving is also not practice. Remember: it is only practice when you are in a similar setting and practice your presentation aloud – in a manner just like you are going to deliver it to your audience.

2. Deep Breathing

The second core ingredient for success is breathing. Now, maybe you are saying to yourself: "Breathing is something I like to do frequently." Well, some speakers talk fast as though they want to complete their public speaking experience as quickly as possible. A fast pace can have a speaker panting three minutes into their presentation. Remember, speaking is an endurance sport. Do not start off in a blur and blow it at the beginning of your talk.

For many speakers, a case of nervousness causes us to take rapid, shallow breaths. All shallow breathing does is make us even more nervous because our system is not receiving adequate oxygen, which is a natural relaxant. We need a lot of oxygen in order to appear calm to our audience. As such, prior to beginning your presentation, and in an area where you won't be obvious, take four slow, deep breaths and fully exhale. This action will assist you in gaining critical oxygen and in allowing you to relax during the beginning of your presentation.

An additional item to keep in mind is planning for deep breaths *during* your presentation. They are easy to slip in during a brief pause, or while the audience is laughing.

3. Hydrate

Before or during a presentation many speakers experience a dry mouth. In order to eliminate this problem, I recommend drinking 8 – 12 ounces of water one-hour prior to your presentation. Something very important to remember is to go to the bathroom five minutes before your presentation. Having to go to the bathroom five minutes in to your presentation can cause a great deal of stress – and, we don't want that.

Drinking water prior to delivering a presentation ensures that our brain has adequate fluids. When our brains are hydrated they perform at their highest level.[2] We want to make certain that we are sharp while speaking publicly.

One more tip: make certain that a glass or bottle of water is handy so that you can take sips during pauses in your presentation.

4. Host Mentality

By bonding with your audience you will reduce your nerves and ensure that many members of the audience are in your corner.

Imagine that you are hosting a mixer. The people in the audience are your guests. Make certain that you arrive early so that you can greet people as they arrive. To the best extent possible, know the core audience so you pitch your presentation appropriately. Shake lots of hands and smile. In other words, seek to build rapport with individual audience members prior to the presentation. Even if you know everyone in the audience, shake hands and greet them. By bonding with your audience you will reduce your nerves and ensure that many members of the audience are in your corner.

4. Be Positive and Optimistic

Remember, no one in the audience wants you to fail. Have you ever gone to see someone speak and hoped that they were terrible? Of course not! We selfishly want speakers to be good so that we are entertained. Your audience wants you to be great –

feed off that. In sum, if you believe in yourself and act confidently, your audience will relax and respond appropriately.

## Segment 2: Preparation

When preparing to deliver a presentation consider asking yourself at least seven key questions. Possessing the answers to these questions can make a big difference between being nervous or confidently calm.

1. What are the needs of the audience?

Picture yourself as an audience member. What kind of information and setting might be interesting to you? This will help you formulate or refine your main ideas, as well as to construct a proper room set up. You may also ask: Do I expect something visual to accompany the speaker? Is my seat comfortable? Do I expect to walk away with handouts? Once these items are tended to, you will be well on your way to providing value to your audience.

Your audience wants you to be great – feed off that.

2. What kind of responses and outcomes do I want as a result of the presentation?

The key here is to strategically determine what the audience will take away with them. As such, seek to list three to five desired results of your presentation. This may also help you develop an introduction that will grab your audience's attention, and craft a conclusion that will resonate with people.

3. What are the physical arrangements of the room in which I will be speaking?

The third question asks you to have detailed knowledge of

the physical arrangements of the setting in which you will be speaking. Some items that come to mind are: Will there be some natural lighting in the room? What temperature does the audience prefer? And, how will the seats be set up? For groups of 30 people or less, I strongly recommend using a U-Shape configuration. A semi-circular or U-shaped arrangement provides an environment whereby a speaker can get closer to their audience. When used effectively, a closer proximity creates a stronger connection between the speaker and the audience.

4. Will I be using a microphone, a wireless microphone, or no microphone?

Determine whether you will be using an amplification device or not. Please note that if you are addressing 30 people or *more* I recommend using some type of amplification system.

5. What if something goes wrong?

The true test of a good speaker is their ability to still be effective, even if things seriously go awry. What will you do if your technology fails? Will flipcharts be handy? How will you handle a disruptive person? What if the audience is non-responsive? Preparing for these types of occurrences does not make you a pessimist. Rather, it makes you able to handle adversity with a cool head. Nothing is more impressive than a confident speaker who is unfazed by the occasional glitches that life throws at us.

6. What questions might be asked?

While it makes sense to anticipate questions, do not get too caught up with prepared answers. The spontaneity and pauses that occur when questions are asked can be an important element to appearing authentic while delivering your topic.

7. Is it appropriate to include examples, anecdotes and quotations?

The use of quotes, examples, and stories is almost always a good idea. These elements tend to bring a presentation to life. Many speakers use examples and stories about themselves in order to create a more personal bond with their audience. This can be quite effective as long as it does not come across as being self-absorbed or preachy.

## Segment 3: Techniques

Now that you know the ingredients to success and preparedness, let's look at 13 specific behaviors to model, as well as items to consider during your presentation.

1. Open with a Zinger

In my opinion, a compelling attention getter at the beginning of a presentation is essential to success. Starting your presentation with a zinger usually elicits a favorable response and relaxes everyone. The surge of confidence generated by an effective attention-getter gives the presentation great momentum, calms the speaker, and reassures the audience that they are in for a treat.

A zinger can be a story, a joke, or interesting information. Recently, I had the pleasure of observing a client deliver a presentation. I love the opening she used. Here is the background and setting: she is in the financial services industry and was set to speak to an audience of 100 people. Her topic was identifying and preventing financial mistakes. While she knew that her core content was good, she also knew that the topic was dry. So with a

Many speakers use examples and stories about themselves in order to create a more personal bond with their audience.

confident tone and positive body language, she began her talk by sharing a personal story:

> "Last year I had the experience of a lifetime – I kayaked down the Amazon River. It is a wild, beautiful river that can be quite intimidating. I was accompanied by four friends who were teamed up in their kayaks. The guide was teamed with me. We observed flocks of toucans and heard the call of howler monkeys. There were several times we experienced turbulent waters. It was during those times that I was glad to have an expert along to guide us. As a result, we always felt confident, enjoyed ourselves, and ended up where we wanted to be.
>
> Well, you may not be heading down the Amazon, but there may be turbulent waters in your future. And I might not be an expert with a kayak, but I am an expert financial guide. So this evening we will take a little journey together and search for knowledge about financial markets that if navigated correctly can lead you to exactly where you want to be."

What I love about her opening is that she started out with a colorful story that provided both compelling mental images and a useful metaphor. She then drew in the audience towards the topic at hand. During the course of her talk she also sprinkled some humor that was just perfect for keeping her audience tuned in and attentive. By the end she actually received a nice round of sincere applause. Keep in mind, the satisfying end would have never happened if she had not nailed the beginning.

2. Organization

The organization of your talk can make or break your presentation. Some organizational items to consider are:

- Preview – will there be some type of foreshadowing of what is to come?

- Review – will there be a summary of what was covered?
- Transitions – are your topical transitions crisp and fluid?

3. Enthusiasm

By showing enthusiasm for your topic you will energize and excite the audience. If you are bored I guarantee your audience will be too. If you are filled with energy and verve your audience will feel it and mirror it.

4. Vocal Variety

Vary the volume, tone, pace, and pitch of your voice during the presentation. Most speakers unwittingly use a monotone voice. This is the primary reason why most speakers are not compelling.

Aside from the five core ingredients to successful presentations, vocal variety is the key to being a first-rate speaker.

When I think of the effective use of vocal variety, one of my favorite teachers comes to mind. He was, of all things, an economics professor. Can you believe it? Economics! What made him special, however, was his frequent use of vocal variety. He effectively used high and low tones, while occasionally altering the volume of his speech. He was absolutely engaging and interesting – even though his subject matter was a hair on the dry side. Aside from the five core ingredients to successful presentations, vocal variety is the key to being a first-rate speaker.

5. Eye Contact

Your ability to comfortably look at people's eyes as you speak will help to build rapport and credibility. Do not look through people while maintaining eye contact. Also, eye contact that is too high (like looking at someone's forehead) can be interpreted as being aggressive. If you have trouble maintaining eye contact, simply look at the bridges of people's noses – they will never know the difference.

6. Movement

Whether you are using a podium (which I typically do not recommend) or not, there is nothing wrong with some smooth, calculated movement during a presentation. When moving, seek to appear non-rushed, comfortable, and confident.

7. Facial Expressions

During your presentation make certain that your facial expressions are varied and that they match the content of your material. Remember, there is nothing wrong with practicing in front of a mirror so that you zero in on the proper facial expression for the proper moment of your talk.

8. Proximity

Use your distance from your audience to draw them in and engage them. It is your job as the speaker to make certain that your audience is participatory. A powerful method of reconnecting with an audience member who appears somewhat disinterested is to move closer to them. Even if you are speaking to hundreds of people, merely moving to a part of the stage that is nearer to non-engaged audience members will perk them up. This technique, the use of proximity, is a useful means to keep your audience alert and engaged. Note that if you are standing behind a podium, it negates your ability to implement this highly effective tool.

9. Gestures

Seek to use gestures that are fluid and controlled. Avoid

sudden or fast movement unless it is emphasizing a point. Also, use horizontal gestures as opposed to vertical gestures. Horizontal gestures are usually perceived as being open or welcoming and thus they draw in the audience. Vertical gestures can be construed as being standoffish. As I am sure you are aware, it is unwise to cross your arms while making a presentation.

10. Visual Aids

When handouts are passed out before you speak, you are no longer a speaker – you become an interrupter.

Only use visual aids that are absolutely necessary. When using PowerPoint during a presentation, make certain that you speak to your audience and never turn your back to your audience while you read a slide on the screen. Also, less is more with PowerPoint. Do not fill up slides with an abundance of words – that is why you are there. Use targeted words with punch, and spice up your slides with visual images.

If you continue to speak after a core PowerPoint slide has been shown, blank the screen or cover the projector so that people refocus their attention on you and your message, rather than blindly staring at a lighted screen. Do not allow a visual aid to overwhelm the speaker. The audience came to see you, not your visual aids.

One last point regarding visual aids: be certain to prepare appropriate transitions that lead from the presentation to the visual aid, and then back again to the core presentation.

11. Handouts

Passing out handouts too early is an error that many presenters make. Unless there is a compelling reason, only pass out handouts after you have covered your material or made a point that pertains to the specific item you are handing out. When handouts are passed out before you speak, you are no longer a speaker – you become an interrupter. What typically happens is that people start to read and leaf through the information you passed out. When you begin to talk again your audience is annoyed because you are bothering and interrupting them while they are trying to read. Don't be an interrupter, be a speaker – at all times!

12. Questions & Answers

Another important item to consider when you are crafting a presentation is Questions & Answers. The first thing to determine is whether or not you want to allow questions during your presentation. If you do, say so right in the beginning of your talk. If want the audience to hold their questions until the end, then tell them so – again, at the beginning of your discussion, not when the first hand is raised.

At the end of the Q & A session, revisit or summarize the major elements of your core presentation. In other words, you determine the final concepts that people walk away with. You reinforce the information or message that you intended to convey!

Most speakers, who open things up for questions, have no idea where those questions are going to lead them. Often the speaker will allow their nice presentation to be hijacked by off-base questions. Then, to make matters worse, the speaker ends their presentation after the last question has been answered. Thus, the audience is left confused or conflicted about what takeaways they should embrace. Don't let the Q & A portion of your presentation detract from your core message. At the end of the Q & A session, revisit or summarize the major elements of your core presentation. In other words, you determine the final concepts that people walk away with. You reinforce the information or message that you intended to convey!

13. Evaluation Forms

Prior to delivering your presentation, decide whether or not you will be passing out evaluation forms. If you choose to distribute these forms, determine the optimal timing. My recommendation is to pass them out just before adjourning. In other words, make your final comments, engage in any Q & A, and then pass out the evaluation forms. Make certain that your evaluation is no longer than one page and can be answered in 90 seconds or less.

## Segment 4: Structures

The next segment centers on selecting a presentation structure that best connects with your audience. Often times speakers will deliver a technically sound presentation, only to learn that it fell flat with the audience. Chances are they selected an inappropriate structure that did not properly showcase the content they delivered. Think strategically about the information you desire to deliver, and then choose one of the six main structures that are highlighted below.

1. Simple to Complex

As the name implies, this structure covers the most basic concept first and calls for more detailed concepts to unfold subsequently. This structure works particularly well with topics that involve science and technology.

2. Timeline

This type of structure arranges events in sequential order. For example, if your company was kicking off a six-month marketing campaign, the timeline structure would be quite appropriate. The presentation could begin with the date and focus of the initial push, and then add date sequential activities in order to bring a visual picture of the desired results into your audience's mind.

3. Problem – Solution

This structure calls for your message to present a problem, suggest a viable solution(s), and then state the benefits of your proposed actions.

4. Propose & Support

During these presentations the main points are stated in the beginning and the body of the presentation provides supporting evidence to back up the propositions.

5. Classification

During these presentations the important items are listed. Then, each item becomes a major point in the presentation. For example, if you gave a speech about a corporate reorganization, you might list each redesigned department and then address each department as a segment of the presentation.

6. Climax

This structure calls for the speaker to discuss main points in order of increasing importance. In other words, the more basic elements of your topic would be presented early. You would build excitement for your audience as you unveil increasingly important and interesting information.

## Segment 5: Post-Presentation Actions

Once you have successfully delivered your presentation, there are two actions to consider.

1. Glance over the review forms that were completed by the audience.

This one-page form should be succinct enough looking so that the audience will actually complete it, and thorough enough that you can truly gauge your performance. During your review pay special attention to the comments that were made. If someone takes the time to write down a comment, it usually merits at least a moment of attention. Also, discount the bottom five percent of your reviews. You will always have some audience members who, for whatever reason, do not think the presentation is fabulous.

Too often we deflect praise and allow negative or constructive feedback to be the only items we retain.

2. Seek feedback from a co-presenter, observer, or trusted member of the audience.

This type of direct feedback is gold. Attempt to flesh out specifics regarding your use of gestures, grammar, vocal expressiveness, as well as your general delivery style and use of visual aids. Importantly, listen carefully to the positive comments and let praise soak in and reinforce the many things that you do right. Too often we deflect praise and allow negative or constructive feedback to be the only items we retain. Do not overvalue negatives. Certainly listen to constructive comments, but do not let praise escape you. By embracing positive feedback and intelligent suggestions we can continually raise the bar and become excellent speakers.

## Bottom Line

The speaking process is something to enjoy, not fear. In addition, the ability to consistently deliver effective presentations to a variety of audiences is one of the hallmarks of a successful professional. By embracing proven techniques, coupled with proper practice, your speaking ability can be greatly enhanced.

## Chapter 5

# Feedback Frenzy

FOLLOWING on the heels of our presentation chapter is information pertaining to the proper use and structure of feedback. Many leaders refrain from sharing feedback because they are non-confrontational, fear pushback, allow themselves to be too busy, or are disconnected in some way from day-to-day operations. Whatever the reasons, few professionals truly deliver feedback effectively. Yet, it is critically important to deliver feedback. A recent study by the Corporate Executive Board validated that providing meaningful informal feedback increases team member performance by over 35%.[3] Considering this data, it would be foolish to avoid sharing your observations and insights with others.

In the movie *Thelma & Louise*, Brad Pitt told Geena Davis: "Armed robbery, if conducted properly, does not have to be entirely unpleasant." Similarly, feedback, if delivered properly, is not entirely unpleasant. In fact, as referenced in the first paragraph, it can be downright effective in increasing performance. It can also be motivating – or de-motivating if

A recent study by the Corporate Executive Board validated that providing meaningful informal feedback increases team member performance by over 35%.

not executed correctly. The following story of Charles and Virginia catapults us into the particulars of feedback.

Charles just witnessed Virginia deliver a sales presentation. She did well. In fact, he is anxious to share praise with her, as well as to give her some constructive feedback. Charles likes helping professionals grow and achieve great results. When an appropriate moment presents itself, Charles takes Virginia to the side and says: "You did a great job!" She beams. "In fact," he adds, "with just a little tweaking, you've got a world-class presentation on your hands." Her upper lip twitches slightly, but she maintains eye contact. Charles then launches into five brief pieces of constructive criticism. Everything he shares is insightful and delivered in a professional tone. By the delivery of the third item Virginia has shut down. She suddenly looks dejected and hears nothing more. Charles walks away from the conversation confused and feeling like Virginia is just not interested in growing her skills.

Have you ever been on either side of this example? Most of us have – numerous times. So what gives? How can this scenario have a positive end? The answer is contained in three areas: understanding human nature, using proper feedback technique, and a mathematical ratio. Let's begin with human nature.

The results of a study about improvement conducted by the Gallop organization showed that when seeking improvement, most cultures in the world focus on their weaknesses.[4] For example, if you play tennis and your backhand is the weak part of your game, you would probably spend most of your practice time attempting to improve your backhand. In a way, this makes sense. The Gallop study also concluded however, what makes us good is not always compensating for weaknesses, but rather improving our strengths. And our strengths often flow to us effortlessly. To use the tennis example, if you have a great forehand, your practice time is best spent taking your forehand to a higher and higher level. In other words, accentuate the positive!

to every extent possible, be specific with your feedback.

Perhaps you are thinking that this is all well and good for tennis, but what about the business world? If our nature is to focus on weaknesses, yet we maximize improvement by focusing on positives, we <u>must</u> find a method to highlight and encourage strengths without ignoring adjustments that will mitigate weaknesses. This leads us to technique.

Well-executed feedback technique holds the possibility of widening team member's receptiveness to feedback and, in turn, breaking down walls that discourage leaders from sharing feedback. The technique that I prefer is a simple and widely-used educational construct called "Plus / Deltas."

As one might surmise, pluses refer to positive work behaviors that are observed. A plus sounds like this: "Virginia, I really liked the tone of voice you used during that meeting. The customer seemed at ease with your presentation as a result."

On the flipside we have deltas. The word delta comes from the Greek word for change. So when we are sharing deltas with others we are not necessarily saying something negative, rather we are suggesting that something could change or be different. A delta sounds like this: "Virginia, when you leaned forward while asking for an additional piece of business it seemed liked the customer backed away. How could that portion of the meeting have been different?"

Please take note that both the plus example and the delta example were very specific. This is an important designation – to every extent possible, be specific with your feedback.

Now for the math portion of the program. The math I am referring to is not complicated. It is nothing more than a ratio really, but for whatever reason there is magic in the ratio 3:1. What does this mean? The answer is: attempt to use three pluses for every one delta. My experience has shown that by following a simple feedback rule of delivering three pluses to each delta, the delta actually sticks. That's right. People are more receptive to altering one piece of behavior or performance when you have taken the time to clearly notice three things that they are doing right. In addition, a three to one ratio of pluses to deltas keeps things positive. If the right team members are hired in the first place, it should be easy to stroke them more than you tweak them. The positive stroking keeps them pumped up and focusing on their strengths.

Charles is now ready to implement his enhanced feedback strategy with Virginia and the rest of his team. How often should Charles share feedback? Well, if he wants a high performing team, he should consider sharing feedback daily. Are there exceptions to his using the plus / delta system? The answer is absolutely! Let's list some:

1. Charles observes a team member who is really screwing up. These instances call for an emphasis on discussing incorrect behavior, coupled with details on how it negatively impacts the team, and what type of behavior and actions are expected in the future.

2. One of Charles's staff members sees things in absolutes. In other words, she wants positives or negatives – but never the twain shall meet. In these instances share feedback in a manner consistent with how the staff member is wired: only pluses or only deltas.

3. Charles' experience shows that different language resonates better with certain staff members. For instance, someone might like to hear "pros and cons," or "positive and constructive." Certainly it makes sense for him to use vocabulary that best connects with his people.

Fast forward: the next week Virginia again finds herself paired with her boss for a joint sales call. Based on her most recent experience, she is dreading the debrief after their meeting. She and Charles cordially greet each other prior to entering the customer's office. Virginia, as she did the week before, does very well with the customer. Charles jots down eight items that Virginia did very well and three items that could have been stronger. After the meeting Charles approaches Virginia, "Hey, you did a great job, may we debrief on some specifics for a few moments?" Virginia stiffens and slowly nods. Charles then shares with her, "I have been practicing new techniques to strengthen my feedback ability. One technique is called plus / deltas, would you be open to feedback, as well as sharing some with me?" Virginia slightly brightens at the fresh tone in Charles voice and the openness of his approach. She gives her permission to continue. "Well, I would like to start with three items that I thought were very positive." Charles then listed three very specific pluses for Virginia. She smiled and wrote a few notes to herself. Charles then said, "May I share one area that could have been different?" "Only one?" Virginia thought to herself. Still slightly fearful she said, "Okay." Charles then stated one area that could have been better, as well as two alternatives for Virginia to consider. He then said, "I have several more pluses, may I share them with you?" Virginia smiled broadly, she liked the new Charles – so did Charles.

What a difference a week makes – Charles embraced a new technique that added structure to his method of giving feedback. Armed with the technique and a heightened focus on strengths,

Charles elevated his effectiveness as a leader and solidified his working relationship with Virginia, one of his top performers.

## Bottom Line

As leaders we must share feedback with our team members on a regular basis. We should give feedback in a manner that delivers the best probability of improved results. By focusing on positives, we can continually enhance outcomes, grow our people, and better satisfy our customers.

## Chapter 6

# Your actions speak so loudly, I can't hear a word you say

AH, here it is, my take on the non-verbal game. Let's start out with a little exercise involving words, tone, and body language. Imagine that all face-to-face communication was distilled into three simple categories: words, tone, and body language. Take a moment and complete the following table as to how you would allocate the importance of these areas. In other words, rate the impact of proper word choice and usage as it pertains to overall effective communication. Then, do the same for tone of voice and body language. Your answers should sum to 100%.

| | |
|---|---|
| Words | ___% |
| Tone | ___% |
| Body Language | ___% |
| **Total** | 100% |

Being the smart person you are, coupled with the fact that the title of this chapter connotes non-verbal communication, you may have weighted your answer towards body language. My experience, while conducting this exercise with thousands of professionals, has shown that a good percentage of people allocate 50% or more of the total to words. Why not? It makes sense since we share thousands of words per day in the workplace. Typically, clients distribute the value of each category equally, but 10% of the time they assign the following values:

| Words | 80% |
|---|---|
| Tone | 10% |
| Body Language | 10% |
| Total | 100% |

The real impact of words, tone, and body language frequently raises an eyebrow or two, and is quite different from what is shown above. According to a study performed by Dr. Albert Mehrabian[5] the actual impact is as follows:

| Words | 7% |
|---|---|
| Tone | 38% |
| Body Language | 55% |
| **Total** | 100% |

Whether or not you embrace Mehrabian's research, his findings certainly add credence to the philosophy of it's not what you say, but how you say it!

All too often professionals painstakingly prepare the words for their meetings or presentations, yet they spend little to no time anticipating the following:

- What tone of voice will best emphasize my words?
- Will my facial expressions compliment the words and tone I will be using?
- What kind of gestures will support my key statements?
- Am I making any gestures that will distract my audience?
- Is my body language powerful or empathetic? In other words, is it consistent with my words?
- What pace will work best for my meeting or presentation?

Suffice it to say that while preparing to speak, there should be ample consideration given to items other than the words you will say. When interacting, the best leaders demonstrate a comfortable blend of words, tone, and body language. As such, we will examine each of these elements.

## Words

While words may only account for seven percent of our conversational impact, it is still important that we select the right words. Certainly if we speak gibberish, our sanity and professionalism will be questioned. In addition, by selectively choosing words that carry impact and imagery we show respect for our audience and maximize our potential to have our message stick.

An item to consider when creating your presentation is the pace of your speech. Make certain that the pace (or changes in pace) that you choose compliment your words and fit well with your audience. Sometimes a fast pace is interpreted as disrespectful, while at other times a fast pace compliments the content of your topic. The same can be said for a steady or calculated pace – sometimes it is perfect, while other times your audience grows bored and daydreams about your sudden demise.

## Tone

Next we turn our focus to tone of voice and just how this plays into effective communication. Tone is interesting because the sentiment of a statement can easily be changed by simply switching the tone in our voice. A soft tone can sound comforting and understanding. Yet, the same statement with a gruff tone can come off sounding demanding and overbearing. Let's review a quick story.

Marty was not happy with Carol. He was disappointed with the report that she prepared – a type of report that he had years of experience in preparing and reviewing. He wanted to coach her so that she would improve. Overall, he liked Carol and believed that she added value to his company. Without planning for the conversation or considering the specific coaching tips he would share, Marty dialed Carol's extension. He was still unhappy, which resulted in an unintentionally harsh tone when he summoned Carol into his office.

While he intended to politely offer Carol a seat as she entered the room, Marty's lack of planning and self-control caused him to say, in a gruff voice, "Sit down Carol." His back was turned to Carol when he initially spoke to her. Carol was agitated by Marty's unprofessional tone and manner. Her discontent was elevated since she was unaware of Marty's dissatisfaction with her latest report. Additionally, she was already stressed because she was in the middle of a time-sensitive task. Soon after entering her boss' office Carol looked quite frustrated.

Marty's tone of voice was still coarse as he began to offer her coaching tips. As such, Carol took offense with each comment. In turn, when Carol responded with questions or comments her tone was caustic and defensive. Neither Marty nor Carol used paraphrasing in order to tap into what the other person might have been feeling or experiencing. The result was a downward spiral whereby nothing was accomplished, save for Carol missing an important deadline. Carol was fuming when she left her boss' office. She soon was venting to her entire staff and preparing her resume. On the flip side, Marty sat in his office: angry and confused.

Have you ever made a statement, the tone of which was quite different than you intended? Most certainly we all have. The result might not have been as extreme as the example above, but likely it was not a productive exchange. The goal, of course, is to minimize the number of conversations we engage in where our tone does not match the content of our words or the intent of our actions.

In my opinion, gauging the quality of our own voice is quite difficult. Remember the first time you heard your voice on a recording? More than likely you asked: "Do I really sound like that?" Simultaneously, you might have been staring at the recorder as if it was engaged in voodoo magic and transforming your voice into something it was not. Truly hearing our own tone is tough, and only the best trained vocal performers have a real handle on their tone. Thus, the odds are good that your tone is not always consistent with your message.

So just how the heck do we gain mastery of the tone of voice that we use in the workplace? The following are five tips to consider:

1. **Ask a trusted colleague or loved one for feedback**. In particular, ask them to describe your tone of voice when you are stressed, angry, or in uncomfortable situations. Chances are your tone may be coming across harsher than you intend in critical situations. Ask for their recommendations and ideas. Also, have them highlight when your tone is at its best. Often times it is

easier to emulate good tone situations, as opposed to being on the lookout for bad tone.

2. **Look in the mirror**. This is an old customer service trick that works particularly well in mastering your tone of voice while on the phone. For a few weeks, keep a mirror near your phone. Look in the mirror while you are engaged in phone conversations. Take special note of your facial expressions. The expression of your face usually mirrors the tone of your voice. If your expression is inconsistent with the words you are using, more than likely your tone is not coming across as you intend. Practicing "correct" facial expressions may hold the key to putting forth your desired tone of voice.

3. **Sensitize**. After you have said something that may have been delivered with too harsh a tone, carefully observe the other person's body language or the tone of their response. If appropriate, ask them if your tone of voice was too harsh. Consider teeing it up this way (with a friendly, inquisitive tone): "Sometimes my tone is harsher than I intend. Did that just happen?" People are often surprised by this candid statement, and will tell you the truth. Listen carefully to their response because their truthful feedback will, if taken to heart, help you improve.

4. **Vocal variety**. Similar to making good presentations, altering our tone can make our words more engaging and elevate our impact.

5. **Be purposeful and aware**. If inappropriate tone of voice is a problem, set up reminder systems in order to heighten your attention to the issue. For instance, some clients have tickled their calendar every day with the simple message: "good tone." Others have made arrangements with colleagues to give them feedback on their tone for a two-week period. The method does

not matter. What does matter is your ability to increase your awareness of appropriate tone and, in turn, use better tone to escalate effective communication with others.

## Body Language

If you doubt the power of body language, consider the mime. "What," you say, "a mime?" Yes, exactly. Think about how much information mimes share with us. They weave entire stories that make us laugh or ponder, and they do so without uttering a single word.

So what do we do with this insight? To begin with we can strive to become better students of body language. Take more notice of what others are telling us by their positioning and gestures. Use this information to alter or emphasize our words and actions in order to best connect with our audience. In addition, become sensitive to what messages we are sending through our body language. Here is another question to ponder: Does your body language reinforce your message or detract from it?

The following section briefly examines the most important non-verbal cues and some of the common and less common interpretations of each.

Think about how much information mimes share with us. They weave entire stories that make us laugh or ponder, and they do so without uttering a single word.

1. **Eye contact.** Good eye contact involves looking at the "sweet spot" – the area between the top of the eyes and the bottom of the mouth. As long as we maintain consistent eye contact in this area, and do not look through people with an unwavering stare into their eyes, whomever we are speaking with should feel comfortable. The lack of good eye contact or frequently looking away from the other person will most assuredly be interpreted as

disinterest or lack of confidence – both of which are conversation killers.

2. **Fingers on chin**. If your chin is being held by your fingers, the other person will probably assume you are interested or thinking. This obviously is positive. If your chin is on your palm and your fingers are on the side of your face however, the other person may interpret this as disinterest or that you are dismayed.

3. **Facial expressions**. Our facial expressions are a big window into what are minds are thinking. A quick scowl during a conversation can cause things to unravel quickly, despite the fact that every other non-verbal cue is positive. As such, practice your facial expressions with a colleague or in front of a mirror in order to ensure that you can maintain a smile or at least a poker face when necessary. Make certain that your facial expressions emphasize the positive information or emotions that you are sharing with others.

4. **Leaning forward slightly**. Often times when people are interested in a topic of conversation they will lean forward while listening. This can be useful in keeping others excited when they are sharing information with you. Leaning forward too much (or too often) when listening or talking, however, may be interpreted as being aggressive and as a result, put people off.

Make certain that your facial expressions emphasize the positive information or emotions that you are sharing with others.

5. **Leaning backward slightly**. This posture can show that you are relaxed. Slightly leaning backward can be a powerful tool when listening to others, as well as during sales negotiations. Leaning back too much, however, can send a signal that you are laissez-faire or disinterested.

6. **Neck Rubbing**. When people are made uncomfortable by something that they hear or see they often involuntarily rub the back of their necks. This non-verbal cue is a powerful indicator of disagreement, and very few people are aware that they ever do it. When you notice others rubbing the back of their neck (and you do not want them to be uncomfortable), I recommend that you consider the following:

   a. Go soft on your tone
   b. Back away from the topic
   c. Redirect the conversation
   d. When the timing is better, loop back to the key topic at hand

7. **Gestures**. Normally gestures are interpreted as someone giving emphasis to their words, or that they are excited about what they are saying. Be mindful of your gestures however, because if they are too frequent or extreme they may distract your audience and dilute the positive impact of your message.

8. **Attending**. This refers to the trident of nodding, good eye contact, and occasional "um-hums" that assure the other person that you are listening. When people feel that they are being listened to, they tend to feel very positive towards the listener. We will cover this concept in greater detail in the next chapter.

9. **Crossed-arms**. This is one of the most significant and most misinterpreted non-verbal cues. It is typically perceived that crossed-arms signal a person's disinterest, distaste, distance, or resistance to whatever is being said. Frequently this is the case. However, on many occasions, people cross their arms because it is a comfortable position for them or they are cold. There are two key points I want to make regarding this non-verbal cue. First, look at a person's facial expression before you pass judgment on what their crossed arms mean. If their expression is neutral,

they might be a lot more interested in what you are saying than you think. Secondly, if you have mixed signals about their crossed-arms or any non-verbal cue that you witness, ask for a clarification. Consider this: if someone mis-speaks or you did not comprehend their words, you would more than likely ask them for a clarification. Yet, so often we receive mixed body language signals and never clarify what the other person is telling us. Asking for a clarification of non-verbal cues is easy, the steps are as follows:

If someone mis-speaks or you did not comprehend their words, you would more than likely ask them for a clarification. Yet, so often we receive mixed body language signals and never clarify what the other person is telling us.

a. Soften your body language
b. Take on a calm, non-threatening tone
c. Maintain good eye contact, but do not look through the person
d. Say something to the effect of: "Ah, (pause) I noticed your arms are crossed. Are you still with me or are you opposed to what I am saying?"

If these steps are executed correctly, the other person will give you an immediate and candid answer – mainly because people rarely receive questions about their body language.

10. **Postural Echoing**. This term refers to mirroring the body language of the other person. It can be a powerful rapport building technique if used observantly. In addition, it can be a useful tool during sales negotiations. When using postural echoing be certain to pause before echoing body language. If used incorrectly this technique comes across as mimicry, which will create a negative vibe and often leads to a truncated conversation.

Earlier I mentioned that it is okay to ask others to clarify the intent of their body language. It is also important to clarify your body language. For example, if you choose to cross your arms during a conversation, let the other person know that you are not closed off to their words or concepts. It is quite acceptable to state in a calm tone: "I'm crossing my arms because this is comfortable – I am totally open to what you are saying."

## Bottom Line:

1. Become a student of others' body language
2. Be acutely aware of the signals that your body language is projecting
3. Practice delivering body language that reinforces your words and tone
4. If you are receiving mixed signals about someone's body language, ask them for a clarification

## Chapter 7

# Don't Listen to What I Say, Hear What I Mean!

MANY years ago I had a "discussion" with a former girlfriend. As the pace of our conversation quickened and the tone began to deteriorate, I did my best to listen to what she was saying. Frustrated, she implored, "Don't listen to what I say, *hear* what I mean!" I stopped in my tracks. After blinking several times I began to laugh. This caused her to shoot me a confused look. I continued laughing while repeating her comment. She began laughing as well, while hurling a pillow in my direction. After avoiding the projectile I said, "You're brilliant! You have just uttered what everyone involved in meaningful conversation desires – to be heard." She stood motionless and then wryly smiled. I continued, "Don't listen to what I say, *hear* what I mean – it's brilliant."

The question now becomes, what are the magical techniques that assist leaders in diffusing heated discussions, hear what the other person is really saying, and also be heard in the process? The answer may be found in the following:

- The Art of the Question
- Listen & Learn
- Power Paraphrasing
- Purposeful Pause

Please note that when the above techniques are accentuated by excellent body language, appropriate tone, and proper word choice, extraordinary results can be achieved. Let's begin with delivering questions.

## The Art of the Question

In our fast-paced business world it is easy to turn into Joe Friday and ask for "just the facts." In other words, it is convenient to ask closed-ended questions that can be answered quickly and get you the bare facts in a hurry. Certainly there are times and places for closed-ended questions and the staccato conversations they direct. If used as a primary question structure, however, closed-ended questions leave an abundance of information in the other person's head – information that if unveiled typically holds volumes of value. Let's face it, information is king in the twenty-first century. In order to be effective leaders we need as much of it as possible.

Jack Welch, former CEO of General Electric, stated that once someone becomes a leader they begin providing fewer and fewer answers and start asking better and better questions. I believe Jack is correct, and your artful mastery and use of open-ended questions will serve many purposes. The effective delivery of open-ended questions will greatly assist you in accomplishing the following:

- Controlling a conversation without appearing in control
- Gaining knowledge of the team member's perspective

- Learning what may be influencing the team members decision-making

Ponder for a moment the words or phrases that begin open-ended questions. If you were to jot them down your list might look similar to the following:

- What......
- Describe.......
- Explain.....
- How.....
- Where......
- Why......
- Share with me......
- Tell me about.....
- Tell me more about.....

Open-ended questions call out for information. They request a real answer.

Open-ended questions call out for information. They request a real answer. It is this fact that makes them critically important, because when you are offered an abundance of information, you have the opportunity to listen. This leads us to our next section.

## Listen and Learn (the art of getting it right)

When we say "listen carefully," just what do we mean? In my opinion, there are five keys to great listening:

1. **Give people your full attention.** Look up or turn away from anything you may have been doing. During conversation, avoid having objects such as desks, stacks of papers, or bottles of water between you and the other person. Years ago I worked with a leader named Barbara who was the best I

During conversation, avoid having objects such as desks, stacks of papers, or bottles of water between you and the other person.

job of squarely facing the person she was listening to. She liked to use a basketball analogy regarding squarely facing people. She would say, “When a player shoots best is when they squarely face the basket – it is their best opportunity to connect the ball with the basket. By squarely facing the other person I create a connection with them.” All hail Barbara.

2. **Be aware of your body language**. Keep your arms uncrossed, tune in to your facial expression, and maintain an open stance and non-confrontation posture. If seated, be relaxed, but engaged. Keep your legs uncrossed and your chair still.

3. **Do not interrupt**. Wait until the team member has finished their entire statement before you speak. This is easier said than done! If you are like most people you desire to dive into passionate or solution-oriented comments while the other person is in mid-sentence. Why do so many people interrupt? In my opinion, there are several reasons. Simply knowing the reasons why we interrupt often allows us to intellectualize the issue and begin to interrupt less. Let’s take a brief look at the foundations of why we interrupt:

- **You are smart**. That’s right. You frequently know what others are going to say before they say it. You inner mind screams at you, “okay, you got it, respond.” Solution: remain calm my friend. Let others finish. It shows respect and sometimes they say something that we did not expect.
- **You are experienced**. You have a bevy of conversational experience and have had similar conversations to the one you are involved in. Solution: sometimes feigned ignorance trumps experience – and this is one of those occasions. Seek to relax and pretend that this is the first time you have been involved in this type of conversation.

- **You like to help people**. As such, you are anxious to get to solution mode. Tactic: seek to temper "solution anxiety." Getting to the solution quickly is not the time saver you think it is. We talk about this in greater detail in a few paragraphs.

4. **Focus on essence not response.** What I mean by this is to pay attention to the essence and meaning of what the other person is attempting to convey rather than formulate what you will say in response. If need be, write a quick note to yourself as opposed to interrupting.

5. **Capture the emotion.** By using your knowledge of non-verbal communication and tone, you can lock in on the emotion that you believe the other person is experiencing. When you finally do respond, your ability to correctly articulate what the other person is feeling will be paramount in maximizing your professional connection with the team member.

## Power Paraphrase

We begin our look at paraphrasing by revisiting items four and five from listening. They centered on capturing the essence and emotion of what the speaker is saying. I refer to the critical action of capturing the essence and emotion as $E^2$. Once $E^2$ has been achieved it is time to leverage the most powerful response technique there is, the paraphrase. For our purposes it is defined as follows:

**Power Paraphrase: Capturing the essence and emotion ($E^2$) of what the speaker said and repeating it back to them using different vocabulary, while modeling appropriate tone and body language.**

When you deliver a power paraphrase, keep the following in mind:

1. Place a slight emphasis on the word that you believe describes the emotion that the other person is experiencing.
2. Use a tone of voice that is empathetic.
3. Use body language that is open.
4. Seek to structure your response so that you are neither agreeing nor disagreeing with what was said, but merely restating the essence of the other person's words.
5. Pause at the end of the statement and wait for the other person to respond. I call this technique a "purposeful pause" and it will be addressed in detail in the next section of this chapter.

One of the best times to paraphrase is when people are expressing emotion in their words due to anger, frustration, confusion, or delight. The reason effective paraphrasing works so well in these situations is that they make the other person feel understood.

One of the best times to paraphrase is when people are expressing emotion in their words due to anger, frustration, confusion, or delight. The reason effective paraphrasing works so well in these situations is that they make the other person feel understood. When a person experiencing emotions feels understood, they typically lower their emotional energy and come closer to being able to engage in a rational discussion. In addition, by helping someone feel understood, you create a special bond with the other person.

Your paraphrase will be most effective when it is tailored to your audience. For instance, a paraphrase delivered to a corporate vice president may differ widely in its word choice and sentence structure from a similar paraphrase made to a truck dispatch foreman.

Some of the words or phrases that typically begin a power paraphrase are:

- You're frustrated because ……
- You sound angered by ……
- It sounds like you are delighted because …..
- So what I'm hearing is…..
- It sounds like…..
- So you think…..

I <u>do not</u> recommend starting a paraphrase with "why" or "I understand." The reasoning for avoiding these is:

- Asking someone "why" often makes them defensive. Thus, by placing "why" at the beginning of a paraphrase you run the risk of putting others on the defensive and causing the conversation to be less open. If you feel that you must use "why" in your question, seek to bury it in the middle, such as: "Please tell me why you feel that way?"

- When we say "I Understand," we shift the focus of the conversation from the other person to ourselves. When seeking to lower the emotional swirl that the other person is experiencing, the last thing we want to do is shift the focus of the conversation from them to us. Instead of saying "I understand," consider saying "it's understandable" or "that's understandable." For example, compare the two sentences below and examine where the focus is for each sentence.

1. I understand how you feel.
2. It's understandable to me that you would feel that way.

The first sentence starts off with "I," which immediately shifts the focus to *your* thoughts and opinions. In addition, do we truly know how another person feels? The answer is "no," we don't. Our feelings are unique to us, especially when they are extreme such as frustration, delight, or anger.

The second sentence starts off with an empathetic tone. The use of "it's understandable" gives us a greater opportunity to have a positive conversation by keeping the focus where it belongs – on the person we are conversing with.

The difference between the two sentences shown above is subtle. You may not believe there is a discernable difference between the statements. In practice however, I assure you that there is a world of difference. Consider not saying "I understand." I guarantee that you will experience more productive conversations as a result.

When a power paraphrase has been successfully delivered the other person will frequently respond by saying something to the effect of:

- Exactly
- Right
- So you see what I mean

The leaders I know who use paraphrasing frequently enjoy hearing some derivative of "exactly" about 85% of the time. When a power paraphrase is <u>not</u> totally accurate, the other person typically responds by saying something such as:

- Not exactly
- Well, sort of
- Kind of
- That's not what I mean

If you hear responses such as these, simply paraphrase again or ask an open-ended question that will supply you with additional details. The following sample conversation provides examples of an open-ended question, a possible response, and the power paraphrase that is set up.

Leader: Please tell me about Ted.

Team Member: We are constantly under deadlines, which create pressure. I try to impart a sense of urgency to Ted, but he keeps moving at his own pace.

Leader's Response: You sound *frustrated* because you are trying to do the right thing, but Ted is not following your lead.

Team Member: Exactly!

Finding out early in a conversation that someone merely wants to blow off steam can be a huge time saver.

There are several notable items contained in this exchange. First, rather than jumping into solution mode, which most of us have a strong tendency to do, the leader paraphrased in order to gain a clearer understanding of the situation. Second, because the leader listened and was sincerely interested, rapport and credibility were more than likely expanded with the team member. Finally, the leader is now positioned to determine if the team member is truly interested in resolve, or merely blowing off steam. Finding out early in a conversation that someone merely wants to blow off steam can be a huge time saver. Think of the many times that you have offered an abundance of solutions to a team member only to learn later that all they needed to do was vent and calm down.

Now we take a look at the next step the leader can take. After the team member has said "exactly," the leader may choose to say something to the effect of: "Would it make sense for us to brainstorm on this issue?" The team member's answer will reveal if they are sincere about a solution or just venting. In addition, the use of the word "us" implies that it will be a collaborative solution. Too many leaders, when faced with an issue like "Ted," allow the team member to delegate the problem to the leader, as opposed to having the team member be involved in the solution.

Thus far we have focused on conversations where power paraphrasing is associated with creating an emotional bond. The technique of power paraphrasing has many uses however. Consider situations when an abundance of verbal information has been shared with you. In order to ensure that you understand the information correctly you may want to use what I call an informational paraphrase. For our purposes it is defined as:

**Informational Paraphrase: Capturing key nuggets of information and succinctly repeating them back to the speaker using different vocabulary.**

The ability to deliver informational paraphrases solidifies understanding, crystallizes in the other person's mind that you are listening, and positions you to share feedback and guidance.

There are an abundance of reasons for leaders to use power paraphrasing and informational paraphrasing. Mastering paraphrasing has the following benefits. It:

- Helps team members feel understood. Once someone feels understood, they calm down so that rational conversation can take place.
- Determines if the team member is truly thirsting for solutions or simply venting.
- Demonstrates that you are truly interested in the topic or their situation.

- Establishes or expands rapport and trust
- Establishes or reinforces credibility
- Serves as an example of excellent communication technique.
- Demonstrates your commitment to the team member.
- Reinforces that you have conviction.
- Creates an opportunity to properly solve an issue.
- Reduces errors.
- Encourages team member involvement.
- Decreases misunderstandings.
- Encourages responsible action and behavior.
- Creates buy-in.

It should also be noted that properly timed pauses make paraphrasing truly powerful. This leads us to the final section of this chapter.

## Purposeful Pause

A well executed pause at the end of a statement or question delivers impact to the listener and illustrates that the speaker is confident. When purposeful pauses are used in conjunction with paraphrasing, effective results are often achieved. For example, after the leader delivers the following paraphrase: "You sound frustrated because you are trying to do the right thing, but Ted is not following your lead," they would pause for four to six seconds and wait for the team member to respond. Keep in mind that it takes four seconds to process a complex statement. A few seconds may sound like a short time, but it can seem like an eternity during a meaningful conversation. Practice using effective pauses during your conversations – remaining silent is tougher than you think.

Another opportunity to use a purposeful pause is after a brainstorming statement such as: "Would it make sense for us to brainstorm on this issue?" The pause, coupled with good eye contact and open body language shows confidence and calls out to the listener to be the next person to speak.

A purposeful pause can be used in many situations, and assist with a bevy of results:

- **Quality responses**. Purposeful pauses give team members time to think. In addition, team members are given time to formulate a more thorough response.

- **Unsolicited information**. A pause in the conversation gives the other person time to reflect. As a result, they often offer information that otherwise would not have been revealed.

- **Questions**. Sometimes, while processing their response, a team member may craft a question or two. These questions are typically helpful in moving the conversation forward in a productive way.

- **Time to think**. You now have time to carefully observe the team member's body language or consider additional open-ended questions that would enhance the conversation.

## Bottom Line

The best leaders possess the ability to effortlessly use power paraphrasing. They ask insightful questions, they listen attentively, they insert strategic pauses, and they connect with team members in a fashion that makes them feel valued.

# Chapter 8

# Death by Meetings

ONE day I was talking with a client. We were having a productive conversation that was coming to a close when she uttered the sound "Uggh." I found "uggh" to be an unusual way for her to end a conversation, but in my business sometimes one hears some odd things. I was undeterred. Without any provocation she then explained that her vocalization pertained to distaste for a meeting that she was about to attend. I asked if the topic was particularly vile, to which she replied that it was just a typical meeting – unpleasant and a waste of time. After I hung up the phone, I pondered the reasons why most meetings are such a waste of time and, after polling mid-level managers in a variety of industries, I compiled this list of their feelings regarding meetings:

- Non-productive
- Wastes time
- Keeps people from doing real work
- Planners and participants not prepared
- Lack of succinctness, long-winded speakers
- Off topic conversations
- Expensive – high-priced talent sitting idle

So how can leaders structure and conduct meetings so that team members do not groan when entering the room? I recommend the following tips and techniques to make your meetings meaningful, efficient, and more interesting:

1. **Have a purpose**. In other words, will you be sharing information, discussing sales, solving a problem, training, brainstorming, coordinating and collaborating, creating buy-in, or communicating policy? Too many meetings are held simply because there is a standing meeting set for a particular day and time. Here is a tip: if there is not an excellent reason to hold the meeting, don't hold one! Liberate your people and allow them to do something productive with their precious time.

2. **State your desired results**. My experience has shown that when leaders formally list concrete outcomes they anticipate from a meeting, the number and duration of meetings dramatically decreases. This is a good thing. Consider this: if you can't list three solid expected results from a meeting, does the meeting really need to take place?

3. **Invite the right people**. Think strategically when crafting your meeting. Be careful to invite only team members who will positively contribute to the meeting. As a result, everyone will benefit from their investment of time and effort. If someone's feelings will be hurt by not being invited, be candid with them. If appropriate, explain to other parties the reasons behind the exclusion.

4. **Start on time**. More often than not I observe leaders beginning a meeting late because a number of participants or an "important" team member is not present. This action sends a crushing message to the team. It punishes the prompt and rewards the tardy. I cannot stress enough how important it is to start meetings on time – even if just one team member is in

attendance. The right behavior should always be rewarded. If you consistently start your meetings on time, it will not take long for everyone to get the message and, begin to arrive on time.

5. **Craft an agenda that is time sensitive.** Sharing an itinerary of topics lets participants know that your meeting has been thoughtfully planned. It also calls out that you expect results. In addition, having designated amounts of time for each segment shows respect for people's time and sends a signal to participants that they need to be prepared and stay on task.

> I cannot stress enough how important it is to start meetings on time – even if just one team member is in attendance. The right behavior should always be rewarded.

The agenda should be quickly reviewed at the beginning of a meeting. Also, you should ask if anyone has any additions they would like to make. By doing this you will avoid surprise topics that could subvert or needlessly extend your meeting. As a result, you will have control over the topics covered, as well as the authority to politely decline someone's addition if it is inconsistent with your topics or would command too much time.

An agenda is such a crucial part of an effective meeting that I have included a sample "staff meeting agenda" for your review:

# AGENDA FOR ABC COMPANY MANAGEMENT MEETING

| | |
|---|---|
| Time: | 8:00a.m. – 11:00a.m. |
| Date and Location: | October 10th in the main conference room |
| Attendees: | Operations, Support, and Sales team members |
| Facilitator /Leader: | John Doe |

Desired Results:

1. Information share regarding new initiative
2. Exchange best practices
3. Enhance communication skills
4. Review and understand data and reports

| | |
|---|---|
| 8:00 a.m. | Opening remarks by John Doe* |
| 8:05 a.m. | Overview and details of new initiative (Steve Smith) |
| 8:25 a.m. | Q & A and strategies regarding new initiative (John Doe) |
| 8:45 a.m. | Exchange best practices (Susan Jones) |
| 9:05 a.m. | Communication review (John Doe) |
| 9:25 a.m. | Practice and refine techniques (Entire Team) |
| 9:50 a.m. | Break |
| 10:00 a.m. | Review reports, feedback, and demographics (David Williams) |
| 10:30 a.m. | Q & A and ideas to refine reports (John Doe) |
| 10:55 a.m. | Summary / Takeaways / Action Items (John Doe) |
| 11:00 a.m. | Adjourn |

* Note: requests for additional agenda items, the use of time outs, and reference to the parking lot will be addressed at this time.

It should also be noted that while the items contained in the agenda will be executed, the order in which they are accomplished should flow in a manner that achieves the desired results.

6. **Look up**. There is no reason why you should read an agenda or a report or do anything with your head down during a meeting. Holding your head up and making terrific eye contact with the attendees sets a positive tone for the meeting, and shows confidence.

7. **Stay on task**. The number one time waster is discussions that are off topic. Shame on leaders who allow these conversations to flourish. The question then becomes: How do leaders stop sidebars without appearing authoritarian? The best way to keep people on task with the least chance of offending or embarrassing them is a technique called "time outs." This reference to time outs is similar to the signal professional athletes make to call for a stop in the action. The best time and place to introduce the concept of time outs is at the beginning of the meeting, just after the agenda has been reviewed. Tee up the use of time outs with friendly-toned verbiage similar to this:

> "If, during this meeting, we get off task, I encourage anyone to call a time out – just like referees single a pause in a sporting event – on whoever is speaking – even me. Remember, if you get a time out called on you (or multiple time outs) it does not mean that what you have to say is unimportant, it merely means that we need to stick to our agenda if we are going to end on time. Does anyone have any questions or comments regarding the use of time outs?"

The best way to keep people on task with the least chance of offending or embarrassing them is a technique called "time outs."

Using time outs and other focusing tools reinforces that you have control of the meeting, are serious about the topics listed, and respect other's time.

8. **Effectively use flipcharts and whiteboards.** Strategic use of visual aids can emphasize important information, reinforce skill building, help ideas come to life, and encourage brainstorming. Don't be shy about standing up during a meeting and writing concepts and ideas on a flipchart or whiteboard. In addition, encourage other participants to do the same. Not only will this add an interesting flavor to your meeting, but it will allow you and others to practice presentation skills in a supportive environment.

9. **Entertain**. You do not have to be a standup comedian, but look for opportunities to add levity or proactive thought to your meeting. People love to laugh. Don't lose focus while searching for humor, but certainly do not pass up opportunities to place smiles on the faces of your valued team members.

10. **Ask appropriate questions**. By asking appropriately timed questions, leaders can flesh out important ideas and thoughts that would otherwise have been missed. Some targeted questions to consider are:

- What are two opportunities that could be created from ____?
- What else? (this one is particularly good during brainstorming or when an abundance of ideas have been shared by a variety of people)
- This is good. Who else has a thought or idea to share in the ___ minutes we have remaining for this topic?

Remember to use a purposeful pause after asking a question. Your pause will give participants the four to five seconds it takes to formulate appropriate responses to your questions.

11. **If it's not on topic, park it**. Prior to the start of your meeting, place a piece of flipchart paper on the wall and entitle it: "parking lot." When a topic or idea comes up that contains merit, but if it was fully discussed would hi-jack your meeting, write it on the parking lot. This technique gives recognition to people who come up with good ideas, yet respects everyone else's time and focus. It also shows that you are agile enough to be open-minded, but disciplined enough to maintain focus during your meeting. Items on the parking lot can be revisited if time permits or given their own separate meeting time, if merited.

12. **Break it up**. If your meeting is projected to last for more than two hours, consider holding breaks every 1½ - 2 hours. Breaks should be limited to ten minutes – I guarantee you participants will not come back after just five minutes. Also, request that people return to their seats within ten minutes – make this an integrity challenge.

13. **Delegate action items**. During the course of most meetings participants either volunteer to complete tasks or are assigned certain deliverables. Seek to have a majority, if not all, of the attendees walk away with some type of action item. Delegation will add substance to your meeting and support your mantra of delivering results. The art of effective delegation is discussed in detail in chapter 13.

14. **Summarize key outcomes**. At the end of the meeting, verbally summarize the key outcomes that have occurred. This action signals that you were paying attention and provides a sense of value and accomplishment to participants. You may also find that participants add items to your list. This signals that they were engaged. The task of summarization calls for you to think on your feet. Many leaders are uncomfortable with this challenge. When you successfully nail a summary, however, you

will not be disappointed by the result. The art of summarization will put your meetings in a class by themselves and assist you in garnering well deserved respect from your team.

15. **End on time.** Just as important as starting on time is ending on time. If you represent that your meeting will last one hour, it is your responsibility to craft and manage the event so that you finish within an hour. On those occasions when the meeting will run over, I recommend seeking buy-in to continue – as opposed to simply ignoring your time commitment and carrying on. Creating buy-in highlights that you are sensitive to other's schedules and interested in remaining in integrity. If your meeting is running long, one way to tee things up is to say:

> "We are fast approaching our time to adjourn, yet we still have ___ items remaining to cover. How many of you would have an interest and the availability to go, say, fifteen minutes over time?"

If you use this technique, keep the following in mind:

- Be honest about the amount of time you may run over – you certainly don't want to repeat the same drill in fifteen minutes.
- Seek to reach a consensus regarding whether to end the meeting or run over.
- Set a new end time.
- Give attendees the option to leave if they truly have other obligations.

16. **Distribute minutes after the meeting**. Since you have already summarized the meeting verbally, it should take only a moment to jot down a few notes that can be transcribed into coherent minutes. Once this is accomplished share the minutes with the attendees and other interested parties within a few days

of the meeting. By creating minutes you are making a statement to the attendees that the meeting was valuable and their time was well spent. In addition, it shows that you are striving for accuracy, as well as effective communication.

If your meeting will be 15 minutes or less, hold it standing up.

Note: the minutes you create should equal about one page per hour of meeting time. If you end up with multi-page minutes, consider creating a one-page cover sheet that emphasizes the major takeaways.

Before we close out this chapter, I would like to share a tip with you regarding short or impromptu meetings: If your meeting will be 15 minutes or less, hold it standing up. I guarantee you that if you hold a stand up meeting people will stay on topic. In addition, I believe you will find that the meeting will be just as productive as if everyone was seated – just significantly shorter.

## Bottom Line

Most meetings do not need to take place. Make certain that there is a good reason to meet. Then, take time to structure the meeting in order to ensure results. Run the meeting in an organized fashion and respect team members' very expensive time.

# Chapter 9

# Facilitative Leadership

HAROLD is excited about brainstorming with his team to develop new sales strategies. He feels prepared to lead a meeting and decided that a facilitated approach was appropriate. Rather than ask a colleague or outside expert to facilitate the session, he decided that his expertise in sales would serve him just fine in leading his team.

He set up the room perfectly. The tables where his team was seated were positioned in a large U-shape. He had two flipcharts in the front of the room, the appropriate level of natural lighting was streaming in, and Harold, already looking triumphant, stood proudly in front of his fine team.

Ignoring any type of icebreaker, Harold began the meeting with a brief comment stating that we all know each other and know why we are here. Then he asked for ideas to boost sales. A bit dazed by his shotgun approach, the team members mumbled in confusion. Irritated by an initial lack of response, Harold began to answer his own questions with his ideas. Since the group was not in agreement with Harold's ideas, they sat quietly so as not to anger him further. The meeting ended quickly and abruptly. Harold harbored animosity against his team, and team members felt as if they wasted time and had been attacked.

Have you ever been in a meeting such as this? Led by a leader with good intentions, but essentially delivered with combat tactics? The resulting atmosphere leading to pressure on the attendees, and awkward silences? You are, unfortunately, not alone.

> When facilitating you act as a skilled invisible hand, while plucking informational jewels from an increasingly engaged audience.

So as not to emulate Harold's performance, let us delve into this concept of facilitative leadership and compare it briefly with the topic of the last chapter: Leading a Meeting. Similar to leading a meeting, yet subtly different in how it achieves solid results is the concept of facilitating. The two primary ways in which facilitating group discussion differs from leading meetings are as follows:

1. When you lead a meeting <u>you</u> drive the conversation. In addition, you freely express your thoughts, your direction, and your opinions. Typically, all participants, yourself included, are seated when the meeting commences.

2. When you facilitate a meeting, however, it is important to remain as <u>impartial</u> as possible. When facilitating you act as a skilled invisible hand, while plucking informational jewels from an increasingly engaged audience. The people sharing thoughts and ideas are seated, while you, the impartial facilitator, stand or sit at the front of the room.

In a nutshell, leading a meeting takes good mechanics, while facilitating a group discussion is an art. A note of caution: when you, the leader, choose to facilitate a session with your team it is imperative that you keep your opinions to yourself. If you begin to direct the group, you will quickly hijack the session and effective results will not be achieved. If you think that you will want to comment on topics, engage the services of an impartial professional to facilitate the meeting.

So with all of this in mind, how can you perfect this art of facilitation? There are a baker's dozen of items to consider.

1. **Review presentation skills & non-verbal communication**. You will need to be on top of your presentation game while facilitating. In addition, your use of proximity and non-verbal communication will be critical while subtly encouraging participation.

2. **State a clear purpose for the meeting**. Let the attendees know if the meeting's goal is to brainstorm, solve an issue, take sales strategy to a higher level, etc.

3. **Be specific on the deliverables**. Prior to or at the beginning of the meeting, share the expected results with your team.

4. **Set up a parking lot**. Have a flip chart page designated as a parking lot. Any items or topics that are off agenda may be placed on the parking lot for review at the end of the meeting or at a later time.

5. **Review the rules.** If you plan on using time outs or special voting techniques, say so in the beginning of the meeting as to avoid confusion during the session.

6. **Break the ice**. Even though you may have a group that has worked together for years, do some type of ice breaker or team building exercise. This action allows everyone to have fun, let their hair down, and relax. In other words, it sets the tone for a productive facilitation.

7. **Ask brilliant open-ended questions**. A good facilitator asks awesome questions. The answers to well-timed, well-crafted questions typically yield an abundance of useful information and ideas.

8. **Lock-in on attendees**. Focus on the dynamics of the audience. Stay attuned to body language and use techniques such as vocal variety and proximity to keep the group engaged.

9. **What else?** This is perhaps the best question that an impartial facilitator can ask. When uttered with an empathetic tone, delivered with open body language, and coupled with a purposeful pause, the question "what else?" will mine golden nuggets of ideas and opinions from your team.

10. **Effectively use flipcharts and whiteboards**. Visual aids assist in emphasizing important information. In addition, they make ideas come to life, and serve as a means for review.

11. **Protect and encourage**. Similar to the section on brainstorming, a good facilitator should protect people who share "fringe" ideas, and encourage team members who offer great input by saying: "Wow, that's terrific, what else do you have to share?"

12. **Summarize**. Intermittently throughout the session, as well as at the end, the facilitator should summarize what the group has offered. The intermittent summary essentially gives the group an opportunity to digest and process. The verbal summary at the end validates that the deliverables were accomplished and provides a window to praise the group for their focus and achievement.

13. **Encapsulate**. Send out a written report which summaries the session. The summary should also share additional praise and ask for feedback and enhancements.

## Bottom Line

Effectively facilitating a meeting demonstrates a broad range of skills. Facilitative leadership is more subtle than the directive approach used when leading a meeting. In the end, the flexibility to direct or facilitate a meeting benefits team members and maximizes the time spent during group exchange.

## Chapter 10

# Electronics – The Road to Rapid Information Exchange

THE rate and pace of information exchange continues to escalate, driven primarily by the ease and connectivity of electronic mediums. As such, it is imperative that leaders maintain mastery of various electronic data exchanges. Note the word *mastery* in the previous sentence. One slip up with electronic media and your words or voice might be all over the Internet – in a not so flattering way. So as not to be YouTube fodder, let's take a look at five areas that are influencing the pace of business:

- Email
- Voicemail
- Teleconferences, Web-conferences, and Webinars
- Text Messaging
- Blogs

## Email: The Proper Habits

Carl is about to send an important letter to a client via U. S. mail. He has taken his time crafting the letter. He preens his fine prose and signs his name. He double-checks the mailing address and finally affixes the proper postage and places the letter in his mail bin. One month later Carl comes across a copy of the letter. He notices a typo. He is mortified. In this example most of us would be mortified. Yet, so many of us are sending out important correspondence via email that contains two or more errors – and we don't think twice about it. Why not?

Email is an extremely valuable communication tool. If used carelessly or overused, however, it can be hazardous, expensive, and cause confusion. Various clients of mine have determined that 2% to 15% of business they lose is related in some way to sloppy or incorrect email correspondence. In addition, according to a survey by Forrester Research, approximately 30% of 294 companies they spoke with had dismissed a staff member in the past twelve months for violating email policies. Thirty-eight percent of companies surveyed said they read or analyzed outgoing email messages. These facts highlight that we, and our colleagues, need to be on top of our game when communicating via email.

So how do we stay on top of our email game? Easy, follow these eleven tips for your email peace of mind.

1. **Use spell-check and a thesaurus.** Certainly you already do this. If not, you are the last person on the planet not to do so. Although spell-check is great, it doesn't catch everything and, alas, it is pretty dismal with regard to correcting grammar. Needless to say, re-reading and correcting emails prior to sending them is a hallmark of a healthy professional. The next two points also tie in closely to this concept.

2. **Print out important client or internal correspondence prior to hitting Send**. Perhaps you are saying, "Hey, Al Gore would be appalled - I don't want to waste paper." Well, I am sorry to bring out the environmentalist in you, but consider this:

man has been reading paper documents for over 500 years. Our brains have become accustomed to and adept at reading words on paper. It is only in the past 15 – 20 years that we have begun to read a large amount of text in electronic format. As such, we don't catch errors as readily in electronic form as we do on paper. If you don't believe me, try a little test. Next time you have an important email message ready to send, print it out and thoroughly review it. I will be stunned if you don't find at least one typo and a sentence or two that you reconstruct.

3. **Find a "proof buddy"** to review important correspondence. There is nothing wrong with having another set of eyeballs review important correspondence. An objective opinion will help you confirm that your message will be interpreted in the manner that you intend.

4. **Do not use email as your only channel of communication.** Yes, it is easy and quick. But if you get too informal or use it exclusively to communicate with others, you will become a one-dimensional communicator. Remember: body language and auditory tone are important qualities to incorporate in communication, and email contains neither.

5. **Be succinct.** Emails longer than a paragraph or two are typically not read right away. Also, use good judgment with regard to when it is time to take your fingers off the keyboard and move them to the dial pad. After swapping two or three emails, especially if multiple people are involved, it is probably time to pick up the phone and talk to someone.

6. **Have a clear message.** Seek to have the subject line describe the true topic of your email. Also, avoid acronyms that might be confusing to part or all of your audience. In other words, state your request or information as simply as possible.

7. **Only copy relevant team members**. Be certain about who really needs to be on the "to" and the "cc" line. Too often people cc far too many people. This creates confusion – for uninterested parties, as well as for relevant receivers. In addition, don't populate your addressee fields until you are certain that your message is okay to send.

8. **Encourage questions or feedback.** By welcoming thoughts and opinions you show that you are open-minded and collaborative.

9. **Take a breath and control your anger.** Emails that contain anger and/or sarcasm are rarely productive. Rather than send them, take a deep breath and a short break and attempt to calm down. Then, pick up the phone or make a personal visit. If you are upset, an email message is typically not the best means of communication.

10. **Keep jokes to a minimum.** I love to laugh – we all do. Email is a great way to quickly distribute fun and fanciful items – <u>after hours</u>. During business hours however, play it straight. Sending too many jokes can dilute the fact that you are a serious professional. In addition, do you really want jokes flying all over the Internet with *your* business signature on them?

11. **Plan time for emails.** It is easy to retrieve and send quick emails on the fly. However, many of us receive requests that take some thought or action prior to responding. Build time into each day that is dedicated to email correspondence. Often, just the act of allocating a portion of your day to email can reduce the stresses and strains you experience. Also, if possible, delegate some of your email burden to another colleague. Conveniently, delegation will be covered in an upcoming chapter. But for now we turn our attention to voicemail.

## Curse of the Voicemail

Donald is excited about the news he just received from a client. He has worked hard and nailed a good piece of business. As such, Donald can hardly wait to share his triumph with colleagues. Without thinking, he picks up the phone and leaves a rambling, long-winded account of the meeting on his boss's cell phone. Several hours later Donald's boss listens to the message. Afterward, he stares at the phone with a flummoxed expression on his face. He ponders advising Donald about the company's substance abuse policy.

Have you ever received a voice message similar to the one that Donald sent? Well intentioned? Certainly. Effective? No way! So why did Donald leave such a career-damaging voice message? The answer is because he did not follow the Super 7 Rules for effective voice messaging. Yes my friends, there are rules, darn good ones if you ask me, for leaving voice messages. Let's take a look at the rules for better voicemail.

1. **Think it through.** Take 30 seconds before you pick up the phone and ponder your desired outcomes for the call, as well as what type of message you will leave if you do not connect first hand.

2. **Make it quick.** These days, most of us are receiving messages on our cell phones so time is money. Also, if you take more than 60 seconds you risk losing your audience. In other words, do not leave voice novels! Tip: after you leave a message, get in the habit of looking at the timer on your phone. A great majority of your messages should be 59 seconds or less.

3. **Clarity.** The audio quality of voicemail is crucial. Speak up, enunciate, and state your business clearly.

4. **Speak slowly when leaving a message.** Consider leaving your phone number twice – once at the beginning and once at the end of your message. The recipient should never have to replay your message in order to get your number.

5. **Give your message a headline.** Help the recipient determine which calls are top priorities. In other words, if you are leaving mission critical information, state that in the very beginning of your message.

6. **Be specific about what you want.** There's a good chance someone can leave the information you need on your voicemail, thus eliminating an unnecessary round of phone tag.

7. **Be specific about when you are available for return calls**. Phone tag drives most people nuts. With prospects, it can be deadly. Let people know the exact timeframes and days that you will be most available to receive their return call. Also, if they do not need to return your call, tell them.

Well, there you have it – the Super 7 Rules for leaving more effective voicemail. Now, what are you going to do with all that extra time? Perhaps engage in a teleconference.

## Teleconferences, Web-conferences, and Webinars, oh my

Ellen receives an e-vite to participate in a teleconference. She cringes as she hits the accept button. Her mind wanders as she ponders just how much productive time will be sucked away as she gets phone-ear while listening to disjointed blather.

A new lease on business-life is just on the horizon for Ellen, however, if, and only if, her teleconference organizer embraces a few simple guidelines. It should be noted that these guidelines hold true for web-conferences and webinars, as well as teleconferences.

1. **Start on time.** Professionals who delay starting a meeting in order to accommodate late comers are penalizing people who exhibit proper behavior by arriving on time, and rewarding people who exhibit poor behavior by arriving late. Even if you have only a handful of attendees, start on time. Late comers aren't dumb, they will get the message and eventually will show up on time.

2. **Introduce attendees.** Take the time to briefly introduce the attendees, or at least the major speakers during the teleconference.

3. **Provide an agenda.** At a minimum share a verbal agenda with attendees. If the teleconference will be longer than 1½ hours send out a formal agenda the day before the meeting. By providing an agenda you will be adding important structure to the meeting, as well as notifying attendees that there is a serious business purpose.

4. **Explain rules and tools.** Some common rules and tools are as follows:

   a. **Mute feature.** Often teleconference attendees are participating in an environment that has background noise. At the beginning of the teleconference encourage people to utilize the mute feature on their telephones.

   b. **Discourage use of email.** Ask people to be courteous and not to view or respond to email during the teleconference. In other words, ask for each participant's full attention.

c. **Encourage verbal cueing.** There is nothing wrong with the occasional "uh huh," or "good point" in order to let other participants know that you are listening and paying attention.

d. **Time-outs.** In order to maintain order and focus, consider allowing anyone to call a time-out on anyone else. As long as it is universally allowed, it can help keep your teleconference on track.

e. **Parking lot.** Frequently a non-agenda item will be brought up and, if allowed, it will hijack your wonderful planned teleconference. Don't let this happen to you. By introducing a "parking lot" for good, but off-agenda ideas, you provide an easy method to dismiss or delay unwanted dialog.

5. **End on time**. By ending on time you show respect for people's time and obligations. If you want to go over the time limit that has been set, get the permission of the attendees. In this case, a consensus must be reached or a follow up meeting should be scheduled.

By consistently following the above stated guidelines you can quickly become a role-model for delivering results from teleconferences, web-conferences, and webinars. The topic of text messaging, however, is a different world.

## Text Messaging

"I feel the burn." That's what Bob said to his peers after being crowned the text message king of his department. The burn he was referring to was in his thumbs, because he just equaled the world record for text messaging, an astonishing 35 words per minute – without any errors mind you.

Text messaging has grown in popularity and in the process has become a big deal. So whether you have hitched up your electronic horse to this bandwagon or sit idly on the sidelines, you should be aware of some hazards and benefits of this frenetic activity.

The hazards:

1. **It's fast**. Sometimes professionals fire off a text message, look at their phone, and suddenly verbalize expletives because they misstated some facts or sent it to the wrong person. Text messaging often catches people when they are busy, distracted, or in the heat of the moment. Sometimes our response is not consistent with our usual manner or language. Thus, our correspondence comes across as odd and unprofessional.

2. **Plain Jane**. Unless your text messages are being run through your computer or server they may not have the professional appearance of your typical email responses. These messages can be construed as rushed or unimportant to the receiving party.

3. **No spell check**. Again, if your text message is not run through your computer or server it may not be privy to spell-check and grammar-check. This can be catastrophic to horrendous spellers, like me.

The benefits:

1. **It's fast**. You receive a message, and next thing you know, you have fired off a response. Just like that – boom, it's done. Nice.

2. **Responsive perception**. Who does not value the perception of being a quick-responding professional? No one, that's who. If you desire the perception that you respond quickly to customers and team members who value your input, then text messaging could be the right ticket for you.

3. **Filled in cracks**. By responding to messages promptly you minimize the risk of forgetting about a message or accidentally deleting it – and thus not responding at all. Any tool that can reduce the odds of something falling through the cracks is worthy of consideration.

So, the choice is yours regarding text messaging. Hopefully, you will feel the burn from your thumbs, not from a red face after sending a sloppy message.

## Blog-a-licious

A web log or "blog" is a website where an article, concept or idea is displayed and then additional entries (comments) are displayed in reverse chronological order, following the original entry. According to a blog search engine called Technorati, as of December 2007 there were in excess of 112 million blogs worldwide. It would not surprise me if the number of blogs doubled within two years.

Blogging is a means of communication that is gaining incredible traction. If you do not already maintain a blog, the concept is worthy of your investigation. Setting up and maintaining a blog is easy. It is something you can set up yourself or delegate to your favorite techno-geek.

The question then becomes, just why the heck would I want to blog anyway? This is a fair question that is best answered by listing the benefits of blogging:

1. **Convenience**. It serves as a convenient method to connect with an array of people regarding your thoughts, their feedback, and ancillary concepts and ideas that are sparked by the resulting interchange.

2. **Broad audience**. It spurs responses from a wide array of people. Because people can respond to a blog, yet remain anonymous, there are great numbers of people who are comfortable participating in blogs. Remember, when the possibility of confrontation has been taken out of communication, the scope and size of the audience skyrockets.

3. **Authenticity**. There is a rawness and authenticity that makes a blog a very real experience. Due to the anonymity factor, people do not hold back. You will receive verbiage that reeks of sincerity and, occasionally, peppery language.

Are there drawbacks to blogging? Possibly a few:

1. **You don't know what you are going to get**. There are a few whackos out there and a nice cross-section of them will undoubtedly visit your blog. Be prepared for a few entries that will make you say "hmmmn."

2. **Minimal editing**. While there are tools that you can employ to edit or truncate certain blog entries, you must be very selective about editing the responses you receive. Be careful

about too much editing – blog enthusiasts can smell censorship a mile away.

3. **Cruelty**. Because people can respond to blogs and remain anonymous, certain respondents tend to be more critical or cruel than they would be otherwise. If you don't have thick skin, don't blog.

## Bottom Line

Communication is king; and mastering electronic communication is paramount due to its speed, low cost, and efficiency. The new big gorilla on the electronic-block is the blogger. Whether you are an entrepreneur or in the corporate world, I strongly encourage you to maintain several blogs or, at a minimum, contribute comments to highly-reputable, highly-ranked blogs on a weekly basis.

# Chapter 11

# The Power of 5 – Getting Your Point Across

"The single biggest problem with communication is the illusion that it has taken place."

—George Bernard Shaw

THIS chapter begins by taking a look at a leader named Robert. He had a vision, and a story to tell. Robert was tired of some of the bad habits and mediocre performance he witnessed in the workplace. He believed his team was much better than the results they had been delivering. Robert wanted to convey his desire for his team to improve – and he had several specific behaviors and results that he was looking for. His message was to be delivered during his team's weekly group meeting. Robert prepared well for the meeting and was optimistic as his team gathered together in a conference room. He did a fine job of creating a positive atmosphere, as well as stating a compelling business case. While he was talking, Robert observed heads nodding in agreement and good eye contact. He was encouraged. "They get it," he thought to himself. Everyone seemed energized as they left the meeting. Many of the team members thanked him for his vision and candor. Robert was on a cloud – prepared to see the kind of performance he knew his team was capable of achieving.

The next day Robert's team worked in an inspired fashion. Robert heaved a sigh of relief and focused on his regular tasks and customers. Two weeks later Robert tore himself away from his personal agenda and took time to observe his team. What he witnessed shocked and angered him. Everyone was doing what they had always done – bad habits, sloppy work, etc. Robert was incensed. He thought to himself, "I know they got the message, they were nodding and looked me right in the eyes during our meeting – what the heck is going on?"

What is going on indeed! Have you ever experienced a scenario such as Robert's? I bet you have. In addition, I bet you were fuming at the thought of your team not responding to your well-timed, well-delivered message. So what's the deal? Why are messages like Robert's not sticking the way they are intended? The answer is simple: we are dealing with people, not robots, and people need reinforcement and follow up in order to effect change.

People need reinforcement and follow up in order to effect change.

So often when we are looking to change things in the workplace, the changes we desire have to do with people behaving differently. Well, to affect new behaviors there needs to be time and reinforcement. Consider someone who is learning a new sport or attempting to quit smoking. They typically do not master a concept as soon as it is introduced. Rather, they have to concentrate, make some mistakes, and practice before their new behavior is realized. Likewise, in the workplace, leaders cannot simply utter a new vision and expect their team to embrace it and run with it. At a minimum the message must be restated. Consider the following statistics:

- People retain approximately 10% of what they read
- People retain approximately 20% of what they hear
- People retain approximately 70% of what they experience[6]

It is the leader's job to make certain that the message that is delivered sticks.

If people only retain 20% of what they hear, and you deliver one verbal message, how can you expect your people to deliver what you ask? Just doing some simple math would connote that the message should be delivered at least five times in order to have any hope of it sticking. This brings us to an important realization: It is the leader's job to make certain that the message that is delivered sticks. That's right. Most leaders believe that once an important message or directive has been delivered they are somehow off the hook, and the pressure is now on their people to perform. This is not correct. The leader is never off the hook and, frankly, is not leading very well if they do not repeat important messages (without ire) many times, and serve the message to their people via different mediums.

I like to refer to the five "exposures" I recommend as "The Power of 5." It is a nice number to keep in mind when you are unveiling new initiatives, praising and reinforcing, or driving change. The exposures can range from verbal exchanges at meetings, to memos, to phone calls, to emails. The important elements are the clarity of the message, coupled with meaningful repetition. In other words, there needs to be passion in our presentation – anything less will be sniffed out by team members and treated like a worthless corporate initiative, not worthy of embracing.

## Bottom Line

By passionately repeating critical information and important desired behaviors, leaders drive home the point that what they are saying matters and is deserving of team-member action.

## Chapter 12

# Small Talk is Big Talk

SANDRA is a capable leader. She has great technical skills, experience, and ambition. In Sandra's mind she is ready to go to the next level. There is only one problem – Sandra is perceived as a cold fish. Her team members, peers, and upper management all view Sandra as a competent worker with zero personality. Her nickname, unbeknownst to her, is "Ice Woman."

In her personal life, Sandra is warm and conversant. Yet, somehow during her career she developed a belief that "business is business" and everyone should focus solely on tasks. Sandra is missing a key communication skill – the ability to make meaningful small talk. In a business world where communication and rapport are paramount, small talk is big talk. Somehow Sandra must transfer elements of her after-hours personality over to her work life. Otherwise, she will find herself stuck in non-promotion land, sporting a wicked nickname. How can Sandra master small talk and put her career back on track? There are eight items for any leader to consider.

1. **Embrace the importance**. Many leaders miss the point that their ability to drive small talk builds rapport, enhances collaboration, and indirectly results in increased productivity. Small talk often

uncovers hidden skills, ideas that are applicable to work, and challenges in the workplace that otherwise would not have been revealed.

2. **Desire and sincerity**. If you have a deep desire to better connect with your people, but simply lack in technique and courage, you will be fine, read on. While making small talk it is imperative that you come across as warm and sincere. A huge part of being perceived as sincere is to possess real sincerity, coupled with the effective use of body language. If, when you begin to engage in small talk, it is obvious that you are uncomfortable with the activity, it will be difficult to convince others that you have turned over a new leaf. Note: if you truly don't have an interest in your team members, and in growing rapport with them, do not attempt small talk. Rather, be aware of the sobering fact that your lack of interpersonal interest is a leadership flaw and a limitation on your career potential.

3. **Be deliberate**. Develop the habit of being conscious of making small talk. Tickle your calendar every day for two months with a reminder to engage in small talk. Then, follow up and grow your small talk skills.

4. **Make a list**. Create a list of open-ended and closed-end questions that you memorize. This list will be of service to you on those occasions when a small talk opportunity arises, and you freeze. Some questions and or comments to consider are as follows:

- When you are not at work, what are your two favorite things to do? Keep it clean now.
- Wow, that's interesting, tell me more about that? (Note: only say, 'that's interesting' if it sincerely interests you.)
- Other than this metropolis we live in, what's your favorite city? Ah, I've never been there, please tell me

about it. (Note: if you have been there, share some of your experiences.)

- Hey, what do you prefer: books or movies? What's your favorite?

5. **Practice**. It will become easier to engage in small talk as it becomes a habit. When you are enhancing or building this skill though, it is best to practice with a loved one or a close confidant prior to testing your skills at work.

6. **Persistency.** You cannot engage in small talk, win people over, and then stop doing it. Small talk is like brushing your teeth – it must be done regularly to be effective.

7. **Wander twice per day**. At least twice a day wander around and mingle with your team members. Depending upon the number of people you connect with this does not have to take a long time. If you are pressed with deadlines, there is no reason you need to spend more than 30 seconds per team member. When pressed for time, or confronted with an overly verbose team member, simply use a closed-end technique such as this: "Bob I literally have just 30 seconds, but I wanted to check in and see how your day is going." If Bob goes on a verbal rampage, after 30 seconds look at your watch, tap on it and say in a friendly tone, "Ugg – Bob, gotta run, but I will catch up with you tomorrow." Trust me, your brief interaction will be viewed positively, not negatively.

8. **Patience**. It will take people a while to embrace your efforts. They will be wary at first and, if this behavior is new, rightfully so. Your persistence will win them over. Be patient.

## Bottom Line

Small talk is big talk and your ability to engage in it will make team members feel comfortable around you, as well as build cooperative relationships.

## Chapter 13

# It could be done, it should be done, it will be done...by somebody else

THIS chapter is for people who have the opportunity to delegate. Frequently professionals think about delegating, but more often than not they refrain. Here is what typically happens: the "delegator" begins to visualize what the task will look like when it is completed. Then they think about what it will take to finish the task properly. In essence, they engage in a heated debate in their own mind during which they falsely convince themselves that "I'm the only person who can do this right" or "it will take me just as much time to explain the task as it will for me to just do it." In the end, the potential delegator keeps the task on their plate. As a result, they continue to be overwhelmed, overworked, and in possession of a not so healthy work–life balance.

In order to improve the delegation process (note that "process" is mentioned rather than saying the "act of delegating"), two big psychological hurdles need to be examined. The first hurdle involves perfectionism. The first step in overcoming this hurdle is to determine or acknowledge the level of your perfectionist tendencies. My experience has shown that a large percentage of people in the position to delegate, possess the trait of perfectionism. It's not a bad trait, but it is something we must wield intelligently if we ever hope to effectively delegate.

The second hurdle is "a lack of comfort with letting people fail." This may seem like an odd statement, but let's face it, most of us are uncomfortable watching people struggle, especially if we could have prevented it by just doing something ourselves in the first place.

The keys to moving toward consistent delegation are these:

1. **Acknowledge**. Admit that, at times, you are a perfectionist and that even though someone may complete a task in a different manner than you or with a different final appearance, it can still be good and useful. Challenge your comfort zone and give others a chance to show what they can accomplish!

2. **Accept**. Realize that people can learn a great deal by struggling and even failing. In other words, consciously strive to become comfortable with people occasionally failing (so that they can grow).

Keep in mind that the skill of delegation is closely related to growing & developing other people. If you want those around you to grow, jettison the psychological baggage that is preventing you from consistently delegating.

With baggage properly stowed, we can now examine the finer points of how to effectively delegate. It's simple: communicate and share your expectations. More importantly, ask what the other person's expectations are of you. The flavor of the conversation with the "delegatee" may include some or all of the following eight points:

1. **Timeframe**. What is the desired completion date and/or time relating to the task you are delegating?

2. **Updates.** How often and in what form do you want to be apprised of the status of the delegated task?

3. **Directions**. Explain the basics of what you are looking for. If the delegatee wants more direction, or if they want you to tell them how to do something, let them ask. Don't insult them by telling them how to do everything.

4. **Point Person.** If you are delegating to a group, make certain that one person is selected as the group leader. This puts the ultimate responsibility of completion on the shoulders of one person and gives you a clear point of contact with the group.

5. **Resources**. What resources, if any, will be at the person's disposal?

6. **Availability**. Will you be available to the delegatee, or are they on their own? Be honest.

7. **Express Confidence.** Share with the other person that you would not have delegated something to them if you did not believe in their abilities.

8 **Cheerlead**. If they do a good job, lavish praise upon them. If they fail, coach them and express confidence, if appropriate, that next time they will succeed.

To help guide you through the delegation process, I have created a spiffy checklist that adds structure to the act of delegating. Consider modifying the checklist so that it best supports your situation and resources.

## Delegation Checklist

Date Delegated: ______________________________

Delegatee: ______________________________

Item Delegated: ______________________________

| Items Discussed | Comments |
|---|---|
| Timeframe | |
| Updates | |
| Directions | |
| Point Person | |
| Resources | |
| Availability | |
| Express Confidence | |
| Cheerlead | |
| Other | |

### Additional thoughts or remarks:

______________________________

______________________________

______________________________

______________________________

If this seems drawn-out to you, you're right. Delegation is more than an action – it is a process.

## Bottom Line

There are many benefits to effectively delegating.

1. It will free up valuable work time that you need in order to complete higher tasks.

2. It will lower your stress level (hopefully) and give you the opportunity to maintain a better work–life balance, which leads to higher long-term productivity and less incidence of burnout.

3. It will help to develop other people. Leaders cannot grow and advance if others do not grow and advance.

4. It will build morale. By showing confidence in others and then giving them praise for a job well done, leaders build group self-esteem and maintain a sense of optimism.

# Part III

# Setting the Course and Creating Buy-In

*At this point in the Leadership Simplified process you have injected agility into your corporate culture, asked and answered pointed questions, and honed your communications skills. You are ready to take your team to new heights. In doing so, you should be prepared to negotiate, set a tone for positive change, and share clear expectations. Success in these areas will create strong buy-in to your vision and values.*

## CHAPTER 14

# The Art of Persuasion

OUT of the mouth of babes come some amazing things - those of you who are parents or who are frequently around "little ones" know this. Recently, my four-year-old son executed the most impressive display of persuasive negotiating that I have seen in a while. In the flash of a moment he delivered a simple question that contained the five key elements of negotiating. In the process he dissolved firm, seemingly-impenetrable barriers. The five keys to effective negotiation that he showcased will be summarized in a few moments. His question and brief story is shared below.

My family returned from a grueling day of fun and sun – we were all exhausted. My wife and I got our sons ready for bed as quickly as possible. Noah, the four-year-old protagonist in this story, likes to receive a gentle back scratching prior to shuffling off to slumber. As he crawled into bed on this evening he requested a back scratch, to which my fatigued wife replied, "Noah, it's very late. It is time for sleep." Noah's response was wonderful. With large, blinking eyes and a soft lilt in his voice he asked: "Mommy, is a minute such a long time?" As my wife's near delirium melted away, she smiled and answered, "No son, a minute is *not* such a long time." She began to scratch his back.

Noah's question and technique contained five keys that lead to successful negotiations.

1. **Emotional connection**. Noah was very successful in striking an emotional chord in my wife. So successful, in fact, that she did something she had no intention of doing. In addition, after my wife finished rubbing Noah's back, she was glad she did. Remember: Facts tell. Emotions sell. Noah's words, tone, and body language sold his idea very well. Please keep in mind, in business sometimes the emotional connection comes in the form of building rapport. Other times it is finding where others have pain in their business and stomping on that pain until they are convinced that you understand their situation and that you hold the key to providing the most effective resolution.

2. **Seek mutually beneficial outcomes**. In today's business vernacular this is commonly referred to as win-win scenarios. Noah found a win by creating a situation where he received what he was looking for, and in the process, the atmosphere and action set the table for my wife to feel good about being an outstanding parent. The power in seeking mutually beneficial outcomes lies in the fact that business, like child rearing, is a long game. Certainly we must all deliver short-term results, but when we lose sight of the long-term we begin to pursue actions that are less than wise or ethical. Long-term, ethical vision helps everyone win.

3. **Negotiate with the decision-maker**. Noah did this quite nicely. If for example he had made the statement to my wife but requested that I scratch his back, I could have easily declined the request when my wife asked me because I would not have been as emotionally vested as she. In other words, seeing Noah's delivery of the request was paramount to being influenced by his words. Consider for a moment some of your past negotiating

situations. How many times have you "sold" the influencer only to receive a quick decline from the ultimate decision-maker – who you never met in person! Why do unmet decision makers rarely accept proposals and requests? Because we allow two important rules of negotiation to be broken. In other words, we did not (a) deal with the person or group making the decision, nor did we (b) create an emotional connection with the decision-maker.

Why do unmet decision makers rarely accept proposals and requests? Because we allow two important rules of negotiation to be broken.

4. **Make certain that the other person gets it**. Noah pulled this off beautifully. He structured his question and the conversation so that my wife's response would clearly state that she understood his request. Her weary reply, "No son, a minute is not such a long time," let Noah know that she got the message. In the business world a technique that works quite nicely is paraphrasing. Remember: paraphrasing lets others know you are listening, and creates a basis for mutual understanding.

5. **Set a time table for a response, decision, or action**. In Noah's case he structured things in a pass/fail manner. He was either going to receive a back scratch or not. In business, too frequently professionals give the person with whom they are negotiating an open window regarding responding. Setting definitive response times and requesting "yes" or "no" decisions are important. Allowing others to "think about it" with no time sensitivity simply wastes time and prolongs the inevitable "no" response.

So, as we come to a close on this important topic, let's review the Noah Method for successful and persuasive negotiations.

**The Noah Method:**

1. Strike an emotional chord
2. Seek mutually beneficial outcomes
3. Negotiate with the decision-maker
4. Test for understanding
5. Request a timely response

## Bottom Line

If you follow five simple steps and remember that everything is negotiable, your team will benefit and you will sleep much easier at night. Who knows, you might even get a nice little bonus before nodding off.

## Chapter 15

# Fly The Airplane—Change Agents

THIS unusually titled chapter is about change. Many leaders get caught up with relating change to the past. Change, my friends, is all about creating something new and parlaying your team's experience into making the "new," magical. Change also challenges leaders to be agile. This is why the concept of agility was addressed way back in the first section of the book. Let me tell you a story.

Many times when I work with groups of professionals I ask them to make paper airplanes. They look at me oddly when I issue my request. Perhaps your expression right now echoes their look of bewilderment. I ask the teams to form groups of five people. They are then charged with the grueling task of crafting one paper airplane per group. They have a ball doing this. Suddenly they are beamed back to elementary school and transformed into delinquent youth fashioning means of flight in lieu of studying math. Ah, but I digress. Each group finishes their plane. Then, they select a "captain" to fly

Change, my friends, is all about creating something new and parlaying your team's experience into making the "new," magical.

their plane. Each captain stands behind a line with their team standing behind them, cheering them on. The captains are instructed to fly their plane and suddenly a blur of white projectiles takes center stage. There is laughter and cheers as the planes settle. The group whose plane travelled the farthest becomes jubilant – thinking that they have somehow won. I congratulate each captain and each team on a job well done. Then I inform them that each plane represents change. There is usually silence at this point. The groups of confused, former elementary students suddenly begin to morph back into responsible adults. I restate that each plane represents change and that it is the charge of each captain to embrace change for their team. As such, they are instructed that each captain, with the aid and support of their team, must pick up the group's airplane and return it to where they now stand. At this point the captains strike a pose as if they were going to run the 100-yard dash. They begin to stare intently at their plane some twenty feet away. Then they are advised that this fun little endeavor has a twist – their feet cannot touch the floor on the other side of the line. Confused expressions again greet me. I restate that when I say "go" each captain must embrace change and their feet cannot touch the floor on the other side of the line that they now stand behind. Smiles, coupled with mild looks of horror flash across their faces as the groups begin to comprehend the scope of the task at hand. I say "go." Groups of professionals form wheelbarrows, human pyramids, they jump on tables, and engage in all sorts of seemingly odd configurations as they begin their quest to pick up their airplane. In the end, each group is successful in embracing change, albeit in different timeframes and most certainly by using different methods.

In the end, each group is successful in embracing change, albeit in different timeframes and most certainly by using different methods.

I ask the team to reassemble and to once again take their seats. They are smiling and several are huffing and puffing. We begin to debrief. I ask a simple question: "you were very successful in embracing change, why?" the answers typically come in a flood:

- We worked together.
- Quick-thinking
- Sacrifice
- Working smarter not harder
- Ingenuity
- Competition
- Communication
- Fun!
- Planning
- Teamwork
- Strength
- Strategy
- We had a goal.
- Time-sensitive
- We were accountable.

I nod my head. Further, I applaud their successful efforts. They beam; and they should. Then I ask them, "Did every group finish at the same time?"

"No," they say.

"So not everyone embraced change at the same time?"

"Well, no, not really," is their typical response.

I then ask, "Why is that?"

- We each travelled different paths
- Different resources
- Different strategies and thinking
- Various levels of enthusiasm

"Ah," I say as I look at the list. The group also looks at the list as I say nothing. We all stare at the list for a little while. I continue my silence. Heads begin to nod. They get it. "We all embraced change, just not at the same time," someone finally says.

"Bingo," I respond. "Based on your past experience, what qualities help people embrace change?"

Everyone's thoughts are percolating by now and they throw out a flurry of answers:

- Some people like new challenges
- A belief that the change makes sense
- Feeling it is the right thing to do
- Involvement or input regarding the change
- An expectation that the change will help us personally, as well as professionally
- There is respect for the person leading the change
- The timing for change feels right

After a pause I say to the group: "If someone is feeling resistant to change, should they feel guilty or look at others in the organization in a resentful way?"

"No," the group responds.

I continue, "Likewise, if a professional observes someone who is resistant to change, should they think badly of them or feel better about themselves?"

"No," the group responds.

"Tell me more about that?" I ask.

"We all embrace change within different timeframes and for different reasons," someone offers.

"Indeed they do," I answer, "Indeed they do."

## Bottom Line

Maintain a healthy working environment amid frequent or constant change by:

1. Leveraging the respect and rapport that you have built with your team
2. Communicate, communicate, communicate
3. Acknowledging that everyone embraces change in their own time and for their own reasons
4. Cheerleading, teamwork, and collaboration
5. Having a little fun!

# CHAPTER 16

# The Modern Day Great Expectations – Working Agreements

LANGDON and Bob are peers who work at ABC Company. They are autonomous team leaders, yet, due to the nature of ABC's business, Langdon cannot be successful without the help and cooperation of Bob and his team – and vice versa. Bob is an established team leader who has worked for ABC for over ten years. Langdon has been with the company for five years and is a recently promoted team leader.

A statistic that Langdon learned during his recent leadership training sticks in his mind: clarity of expectations, coupled with a desire for flawless implementation leads to better than a 30% improvement in team member performance.[7] On the other hand, a variety of questions burn in Bob's mind as he ponders Langdon and his new role of leading a critically important team:

Clarity of expectations, coupled with a desire for flawless implementation leads to better than a 30% improvement in team member performance.

1. How can Langdon and I best collaborate?
2. How can we avoid stepping on each other's toes?
3. How can we speed up our collaborative learning curve?
4. How can we ensure that our teams work together as efficiently as possible?
5. How do we achieve all of this as quickly as possible?

What they need is a platform to determine and effectively articulate to each other exactly how they prefer to communicate and collaborate in the workplace.

Ultimately, time and experience will play a part in their success. However, with business moving at a breakneck pace, upper management does not possess the patience for these two leaders to build a relationship over months or years. What Bob and Langdon long for is business pixie dust that magically propels their working relationship forward and upward. What they need is a platform to determine and effectively articulate to each other exactly how they prefer to communicate and collaborate in the workplace. The answer to Langdon and Bob's effectiveness dreams is a construct called a "working agreement."

Working agreements are a communication tool that may be utilized between all levels within a company to foster a better understanding of expectations that leads to increased performance. The key to crafting a working agreement is to allow for a free flow of dialogue. In other words, if a participant in the working agreement process can feel empowered, the odds are good that they will engage in an honest, candid exchange of expectations.

Ideally, a working agreement is an informal arrangement, as opposed to being a part of an individual's personnel file. There are circumstances, however, when it is appropriate to include a signed working agreement in a staff member's human resources file. The beauty of a working agreement though, is that they may be used in all types of situations.

The manner in which a working agreement can be used includes, but is not limited to the following:

- Two individuals who are peers (whether a new working relationship or an established one)
- A superior and a subordinate (again, whether a new or established working relationship)
- An individual and a group, team, department, or region
- Two teams (whether the teams are forming, storming, norming, or performing)
- Situations where individuals or groups are separated geographically and conduct a majority of their interaction via teleconference.
- Situations where a good relationship exists and the individuals/teams are seeking to move to a higher level of performance.
- Situations when an individual or a team is underperforming or misbehaving and corrective action is sought.

It should be noted that Langdon and Bob have job descriptions and they know what broad results each other are supposed to achieve. What they do not know is what each of them expects of the other during the journey of delivering results. Getting derailed on the journey can have a severely negative impact on the results generated.

Langdon and Bob have job descriptions and they know what broad results each other are supposed to achieve. What they do not know is what each of them expects of the other during the journey of delivering results. Getting derailed on the journey can have a severely negative impact on the results generated.

Let's assume for a moment that during the path of promotion Langdon was exposed to the skill of creating a working agreement.

As such, Langdon is well-positioned to introduce Bob to the concept, and subsequently lead him through the working agreement process. As an aside, the working agreement process can also be led quite effectively by an objective third party such as a human resources associate, a sales manager, or an outside facilitator.

The following outlines the steps that Langdon and Bob engaged in during the course of forging their working agreement.

**Step 1:** Langdon approached Bob to see if he was interested in creating a working agreement. Langdon's initial comment to Bob was something like this:

"Bob, recently I learned about something called a working agreement – it's all about sharing expectations and working smarter. Would you have an interest in creating a working agreement between us so that we can have the best working relationship possible? Our initial meeting will take 45 minutes to one hour."

Since Bob is a good professional he agreed to the process. If Bob had declined, Langdon would have learned a great deal about what their future working relationship would look like. If Bob was not open to crafting a working agreement, Langdon would have been well advised to seek intervention from human resources in order to gain advice on how best to collaborate with Bob.

**Step 2**: Langdon explained the working agreement process and thoroughly fleshed out Bob's questions. They set a day and time to meet and begin dialog.

**Step 3**: They met on the agreed upon day and time. At the very beginning of the meeting Langdon reinforced his desire to have the most powerful working relationship possible with Bob and his team. Langdon expressed sincere confidence that the process will be successful.

**Step 4**: Langdon placed several pieces of flipchart paper on the wall and entitled one section: Bob's Expectations of Langdon. He labeled another section: Langdon's Expectations of Bob.

**Step 5**: Langdon asked Bob what he expects of him. At first Bob listed only a few items such as "open and honest communication," "be supportive," and "do your job." In a professional and encouraging tone Langdon prompted Bob forward. He also frequently used the phrase, "what else?" in order to keep Bob thinking about his real expectations. Langdon informed Bob that there is no right or wrong number of expectations - only Bob's honesty will lead to the best number. Bob nods, thinks for a moment, and lists several additional items such as: "return my calls or emails within two hours," "drop everything if one of my team members needs you," and "be available 24/7." Langdon listed each additional item without offering pushback in any form. Langdon continued to prompt Bob by using the "what else?" technique. Langdon also encouraged Bob to list any pet peeves – it is important to flesh these out as they are often the source of arguments or misunderstandings in the workplace. Bob finally finished and is surprised that he listed 39 items.

**Step 6**: Langdon respectfully asked Bob's permission to share his expectations of Bob: "Thank you for being candid about your expectations of me, are you open to me listing my expectations of you?" Without hesitation Bob agreed.

**Step 7**: Langdon began to jot down his expectations – many of them were similar to Bob's expectations of him. After Langdon's expectation of: "copy me on all written correspondence to my team members," Bob began to bristle and object. Langdon did a great job of calmly deferring Bob's pushback. He then acknowledged that in a few moments Bob will be able to ask questions regarding any and all items listed. Bob relaxed and allowed Langdon to continue.

**Step 8**: Langdon completed his list, which tallied 34 expectations. He also complimented Bob for having the patience to listen to the entire list without interrupting.

**Step 9**: Langdon checked-in with Bob and asked him, "Do you think this exercise is a good use of your time?" Bob responded by stating that he found it interesting and desired to continue with the process.

**Step 10**: Langdon told Bob he was going to give him some "get out of jail free cards." Bob laughed. Langdon explained that Bob could now get rid of any expectation that Langdon has on his list. Bob was flummoxed. "Anything?" he asked. "Anything," Langdon answered. Bob smiled and mentioned two items. Langdon circled the items.

**Step 11**: Langdon stepped back and looked at the circled items. He pointed to the one that he was least passionate about – he wanted to start their discussion with an item that was not overly controversial. In a professional and non-confrontational tone Langdon stated "please tell me more about this one." Note: Langdon avoided saying "*Why* do you want to get rid of this expectation?" He remembered that the use of "why" at the beginning of a question can make the other person feel defensive. Langdon knew that it was imperative that both parties felt comfortable and remained as calm as possible during the process of crafting a working agreement. Langdon remembered that by remaining comfortable and calm, there was a greater probability that a productive, intellectually-based discussion would take place.

**Step 12**: Langdon listened carefully to Bob's point of view. Once Bob finished, Langdon paraphrased what he heard. After Bob said "exactly," Langdon asked a clarification question and then expressed his point of view.

One of the powerful outcomes of the exercise is to flesh out areas of future tension.

**Step 13**: After a healthy discussion, Langdon had deleted or retained the circled items – as agreed to by both parties. During the conversation, Langdon highlighted that it was perfectly acceptable for he and Bob to retain an item on which they "agreed to disagree." Langdon emphasized that it was critically important to address controversial items because those are the type of items that could cause heated disagreements down the road. He stated that part of the working agreement process is to root out potential hot buttons and mitigate them. In other words, one of the powerful outcomes of the exercise is to flesh out areas of future tension. What better a place to do so than engaging in an intellectually-based discussion in a neutral environment? By the end of this step Bob appeared comfortable with Langdon's expectations.

**Step 14**: Langdon was ready to re-address Bob's expectations of him. With a friendly tone and open body language Langdon asked Bob: "Now that we have addressed my expectations of you, would you be interested in giving me a few of those get out of jail free cards as they pertain to your expectations of me?" Bob smiled and nodded in the affirmative.

**Step 15**: Marker in hand, Langdon circled three items with which he had a question or an objection. As he circled the first item Bob began to speak up. Langdon remained calm and in a friendly tone stated, "Please wait a moment, I'll be finished in one minute and then you can share your thoughts and opinions with me." Once finished, Langdon sat down and gave Bob his full attention.

**Step 16**: Bob shared some terse feedback regarding one of the items that Langdon highlighted. Langdon listened to the entire message and used paraphrasing to calm Bob, and to establish mutual understanding regarding the item. Bob's tone softened and he acknowledged that Langdon understood his point of view. After they discussed the item they decided to "agree to disagree." Again, they uncovered a future source of tension or argument.

**Step 17**: Having completed their detailed discussion of each other's expectations, Langdon stepped back and admired the list. He then turned to Bob and asked him a question: "Do you have any additional items for either list?" Bob scanned the potpourri of items that were listed and then stated that he was satisfied. Langdon again asked, "Has this been a good use of your time?" "Definitely," replied Bob.

**Step 18**: As Langdon began to pull down the flipchart pages he mentioned to Bob: "If you don't mind, I will type these up so that we can review them one last time before we sign off on them."

Bob looked curious, "Sign off on them?" he asked.

"Yes," Langdon said smiling. "Remember at the beginning when I was explaining the process? Perhaps your eyes were glazing over by the time I got to the part where the brainstorming pages are converted to a professional looking document, and we commit our signatures to it. I believe that there is power in signing your name to something – it shows a seriousness and commitment to working well together."

"I remember now," Bob answered. "I have no problem with showing my commitment to this process."

"Great," Langdon said. "How about meeting with me again in three days for about fifteen minutes? We can review our expectations, enhance them as necessary, sign off, and begin to implement our agreement."

**Step 19**: Three days later Bob and Langdon met and reviewed their expectations of each other. The Working Agreement document that Langdon typed up is shown below. The additional steps involved in the working agreement process are listed after Bob and Langdon's agreement.

## Working Agreement for
## Bob Smith and Langdon James

On (Date), Bob Smith and Langdon James shared their working relationship expectations of each other. It is acknowledged that each professional possesses a unique leadership style. In addition, both Langdon and Bob are responsible for different deliverables to the ABC Company. The bottom line is this: they both desire a strong and positive working relationship. As such, they affirm that they will seek to stay in integrity with regard to the following expectations:

Bob Smith's Expectations of Langdon James:

- Open and honest communication
- Return my calls and/or emails within two hours
- Drop everything if one of my team members needs you
- Be available 24/7 – we "agree to disagree"

- Communicate with me directly, not through someone else
- Look at all sides of a story prior to making a decision
- Supportiveness
- Build relationships with my team members
- Provide specific feedback
- Lead by example
- Be receptive to change
- Respect others
- Be a motivator
- Agility
- Build trust
- Leave personal life at home
- Hold people accountable
- High sense of urgency
- Increase collaboration between our teams
- Proactively coach and manage
- Honesty
- Cooperation
- Address situations promptly
- Thoroughness
- Efficiency
- Share information in a timely manner
- Be professional and courteous
- Camaraderie
- Educate
- Open-mindedness
- No finger pointing – be accountable
- No gossip
- Be approachable
- Respect time
- Good work ethic
- Provide back-up and support
- Positive attitude
- Integrity

- Do whatever it takes

Langdon James' Expectations of Bob Smith:

- Be upbeat and enthusiastic
- Be optimistic
- Smile
- Copy me on all written correspondence to my team members
- Be a good listener
- Collaborate
- Have common courtesy
- Positive attitude
- Provide motivation
- Teach and coach
- Integrity
- Be caring and empathetic
- Responsiveness/Promptness
- Humor/Fun
- Finish assignments
- Hit production numbers
- Friendship/guidance/self-improvement
- Respect
- Patience to a point
- Flexibility
- Direct communication – first call me, then email me (we "agree to disagree")
- Follow through
- Layout the facts
- Encouragement
- Team lunches (quarterly)
- Acknowledgement of successes
- Give the benefit of the doubt (within reason)
- Responsiveness
- Be accountable

- Share constructive criticism
- Receive constructive criticism
- Keep things in perspective
- Grow and develop
- Lead with passion

I have willingly entered into this working agreement and pledge to remain in integrity regarding the expectations contained therein. In addition, I agree to meet with my collaborative partner on a regular basis in order to share and receive feedback, as well as to enhance this agreement as appropriate.

| Bob Smith | Langdon James |
|---|---|
| __________________ | __________________ |
| __________________ | __________________ |
| Date | Date |

**Step 20**: Bob mentioned that he really liked Langdon's use of the word "integrity" in their sign off statement. He stated that there is an analogy of integrity that he likes to explain to his team. Bob mentioned that the explanation seems to help the concept of integrity stick with team members. Langdon asked Bob to share the analogy with him. Bob walked over to a whiteboard in the conference room and drew a picture of a house. In the middle of the house he drew an "i." One foot away from the house he drew another "i." He turned to Langdon and said: "Integrity is a pass/fail concept. You are either in it or not." Bob turned and pointed to the "i" inside the house. "When we are in integrity it is just like being in a nice, warm house. We are comfortable and relaxed – we have done what we said we were going to do – we have met our commitments." Bob then pointed to the "i" outside the house. When we are out of integrity, however, the situation is different. We are uncomfortable because we know we have not met our commitments - it is a place of "ic." Langdon smiled

with Bob's use of the sound "ic." As he stated ic, Bob added the letter "c" to form "ic." Bob then continued, "so before we are out of integrity there is something very important we need to do." Bob added letters behind the "c" in order to form the word "communicate." Bob then erased the "i" and said "Communicate! When we communicate before we are out of integrity we can advise a colleague or our team members of just how or when we will be in integrity. If they accept our explanation we never go out of integrity in the first place. Doing what we say we are going to do, coupled with proactive communication are the keys to a warm, comfortable house." Langdon smiled and gallery clapped, as Bob gave a mock bow. Looking at Langdon, Bob said, "you have my full permission to use this construct – with proper royalties, of course."

**Step 21**: Bob and Langdon then signed and dated their working agreement.

**Step 22**: "With regard to follow up," Langdon said, "why don't we meet for thirty minutes in three weeks in order to review and affirm our working agreement? We can check in and see if we are in integrity or in that icky place." Bob laughed and agreed.

**Step 23**: Three weeks later Langdon and Bob met again. They both had done a good job of staying in integrity. They discussed one situation that touched on one of their "agree to disagree" areas. Langdon had chosen to do something his way, rather than the method that Bob preferred. Bob mentioned that while he was not happy with Langdon at that moment, he appreciated the fact that Langdon contacted him beforehand and communicated what was going on how he was going to handle it. Both leaders agreed that tension was minimized as a result of the communication and the awareness of the hot button. Bob was also surprised that during the follow up discussion both he and Langdon added a few items to their lists.

**Step 24**: Langdon agreed to update the working agreement so that they could resign it. They both initialed the enhancements to the agreement in the meantime. Also, a twenty minute follow up meeting was set for one month down the road.

**Step 25**: As their working relationship flourished, the two leaders used the agreement as a collaboration guide and a communication tool. They continued to engage in short meetings every month in order to review and enhance the agreement. In addition, they were diligent about reinforcing the positive behavior that they witnessed with each other. Finally, they shared the concept with each member of their team and encouraged them to use the tool in order to strengthen their working relationships.

As their working relationship flourished, the two leaders used the agreement as a collaboration guide and a communication tool.

While their real names are different, Bob and Langdon are not make-believe. Their example is quite real. Additionally, three years after they met, and a promotion each to show for their great results, they still collaborate and use their working agreement!

Before the closing comments for this chapter, let's succinctly review the steps to crafting an effective working agreement:

**Step 1:** Approach the person or group with which you desire to elevate your business relationship and ask them if they are interested in crafting a communication tool with you.

**Step 2**: Explain the Working Agreement process to them and thoroughly flesh out their questions.

**Step 3**: Set a day and time to meet. At the beginning of

the meeting reinforce your desire to have a powerful working relationship with the individual/group. Express a sincere confidence that the process will be successful.

**Step 4**: Place several pieces of flipchart paper on the wall and entitle one section with their expectations of you, and another section with your expectations of them.

**Step 5**: Ask them what they expect of you. List what they say without offering pushback in any form. Prompt them forward (in a soft, encouraging tone) by using the phrase, "what else?"

**Step 6**: Ask their permission for you to share your expectations of them.

**Step 7**: Once permission is granted, list your expectations of them. Note: calmly defer any pushback they offer and acknowledge that they will be able to question any and all items listed.

**Step 8**: Thank them for having the patience to listen to all of your expectations without interrupting.

**Step 9**: Check-in with the other party to ensure that they think the process is a good use of time.

**Step 10**: Give them some "get out of jail free cards" and then circle items with which they have questions or objections.

**Step 11**: Respectfully ask the other party to explain their reasoning behind their questions or objections.

**Step 12**: Paraphrase and ask clarification questions as appropriate.

**Step 13**: Discuss appropriate items and reach a consensus regarding the expectations of the other party. Note: it is perfectly acceptable for the parties to "agree to disagree" on certain items.

**Step 14**: Ask permission to share your questions or objections regarding their expectations of you.

**Step 15**: Once permission is granted circle the items with which you have a question or objection.

**Step 16**: Discuss items with which you have questions or objections. Calmly address any pushback you receive during the discussion.

**Step 17**: Review each other's list and add, delete or modify items as necessary.

**Step 18**: Type up the official working agreement.

**Step 19**: During a meeting three days later, review the working agreement with the other party.

**Step 20**: Discuss integrity.

**Step 21**: Sign and date the working agreement.

**Step 22**: Set a follow up meeting for three weeks hence.

**Step 23**: During the follow up meeting enhance and affirm the working agreement. Note: be certain to reinforce positive behavior.

**Step 24**: Update and resign the agreement as appropriate. Set a follow up meeting for one month hence.

**Step 25**: Ongoing: implement, communicate, reinforce positive behavior, enhance the agreement as appropriate, and share the concept with other team members.

## Bottom Line

My experience in working with professionals and teams across the country has shown that one of the best outcomes of the working agreement process is the heightened level of understanding expectations. This understanding leads directly to increased collaboration and, you guessed it, enhanced productivity.

# PART IV

# Measures, Metrics, and Structure

*An enhanced communication style, coupled with a team that clearly understands roles and responsibilities, places leaders on the cusp of heightened success. It is now time to insert proper measures and metrics, along with a corporate structure that matches your team's strengths with marketplace potential.*

## CHAPTER 17

# The Dashboard Lights

MANY leaders ask me what is the secret to keeping their fingers on the pulse of their organization. My short answer is almost always "communication," but just what type of communication varies from organization to organization. A general communication tool that can help leaders stay on top of their organization's performance is called a "dashboard."

What is a dashboard? It is a collection of four to six critical pieces of information that tell you all about how you are driving your organization. Unlike the standardized dashboard in automobiles, dashboards in business can vary widely from company to company, and even from department to department.

### A Comparison

Way back when, there was a drugstore company called Eckerd Drugs – I worked for them while I was attending college. Across the street was our competitor, Walgreens. One of the items that Eckerd tracked on their dashboard was profit-by-store. It was the measure that alerted them to build additional stores in an area. By contrast, Walgreens, which also needed a predictor for store expansion, used a more detailed measure called profit-by-customer.[8] By closely monitoring this measure, Walgreens charted the course of their store expansion strategy. At times, they would build a new store just blocks from an existing store. Why? Because their dashboard told them they could serve more customers, and make more overall profit if they expanded in this manner. Eckerd on the other hand, never really did a thorough self-examination in order to determine if some refined dashboard ingredients would make sense for them.

Where are they today? Walgreens is a highly-regarded market leader, while Eckerds is, well, dust. Did an effective dashboard make the difference? Not entirely, but it certainly provided Walgreens with an accurate compass that pointed them in a successful direction.

## Items to Consider

So what kind of items should be on your organization's dashboard? Some items to ponder include the following:

- Goals versus actual results with regard to revenues, operating profit, net profit, and selected expenses.
- Year-to-date revenue, profit, and expense comparisons with last year and the year prior.
- Per employee revenue and net profit compared with last year and the year prior.
- Customer service metrics versus goal.
- Revenue spikes within a given time period following advertising, public relations, or marketing campaigns.

Are there different items that should be included on your dashboard? You bet – they are the unique items that differentiate you from your competitors. How do you determine those unique items? Brainstorm with your team, talk with strategic allies, and efficiently analyze your marketplace.

### Format

The look and feel of your organization's dashboard should reflect your corporate culture. Graphs, colors, screen positioning, and size of text should all be considered when determining a format. What is important is that your company's dashboard can be accessed quickly, and comprehended at a glance.

## Bottom Line

By truly understanding and accurately measuring the unique properties of your business, you can effectively drive team member behavior and, in the process, differentiate your business from your competitors. Who knows, you might even turn into the Walgreens of your market area. How do you determine these unique measures? Think creatively, and then drive smart!

## Chapter 18

# Lone Wolves Will Die, Alone – Matrix Management

CHANCES are the organizational chart that your business has created is traditional-looking. Probably it is a typical chain-of-command document. It would make sense since this type of structure has been the norm for hundreds of years – it is a quintessential military structure. A traditional chain of command organizational chart connotes an easy-to-understand structure with top-down authority lines. Some organizations, and not always large ones, actually function quite differently from their depicted authority structure.

Reflect for a moment on the chapter addressing working agreements. The two leaders highlighted in that chapter were dependent upon one another for success, yet they were autonomous from each other. Neither had any authority over the other, but they each relied heavily on their colleague's success for their own success. This situation, two leaders dependent upon the other, yet working in different organization silos, is typical of matrix management.

If we delve deeper into a matrix-structured organization, we witness entire silos of people who possess different areas of responsibility – with no authority over colleagues who they depend upon for success. A classic example of this dynamic is what I call "the sales manager / service manager continuum." In many companies the sales manager cannot be successful without solid service after the sale. Similarly, the service manager cannot lead a thriving department without a steady influx of new customers. These professionals need each other. However, due to the divergent skills requirements of their jobs, they are typically peers, with similar organizational titles – neither one possessing the corporate authority to boss the other around. What usually happens? Answer: conflict and battle.

The sales and service managers referenced above are trapped in a matrix organization. The funny thing is many times they don't even realize it. Moreover, their organizational chart typically does not accurately depict their relationship. So how do these leaders, and others like them, work effectively within a matrix organization? In a word, collaboration. There are two elements of collaboration that are crucial in a matrix environment:

- Frequent communication
- Sharing expectations

Any leader working in a matrix would be well advised to master the communication skills covered in section two of this book. My further advice is to become a wizard at initiating and brokering working agreements – they are a fabulous tool for amicably sharing and receiving expectations.

If ever there was a time for a leader to walk the talk regarding collaboration, it is when they are ensconced in a matrix management structure. Leaders who are embroiled in a matrix, but who do not collaborate, easily stand out as lone wolves. And if you have ever watched Animal Planet's program about wolves, you know that pack animals who become lone wolves die alone – and quickly. Don't be a lone wolf, figure out other ways to stand out in your organization.

## Bottom Line

Take an objective look at your business and examine pragmatic organizational structures. Craft a visual picture of the structure that accurately portrays your business world. Get team input during the process. Then communicate the structure with team members and emphasize collaboration. Lead by example. By and large, people crave structure, communication, and empowerment – give it to them.

CHAPTER 19

# The Business of Swarm Theory

A school of mackerel senses a predator. Each individual pays close attention to their neighbor, so information travels rapidly through the pack. The predator closes in, but the group stays calm, yet alert. They stick together, change direction quickly while avoiding collisions, and move in the same direction. Result: a confused, exhausted predator that chooses to expend its energies elsewhere.

Yes, yes, I have been watching a lot of Animal Planet lately. Is that such a bad thing? But there is so much we can learn from nature – even lessons that pertain to the business world.

In the previous chapter we examined matrix management and the importance of collaboration. Well, swarm theory is collaboration in action. In addition, it contains the intrigue of a phenomenon called swarm intelligence.

Consider ants. They have division of labor: scouts, foragers, workers, soldiers, and let us not forget their leader, the queen. Yet when their scouts spot food (opportunity) or trouble (increasing competition) the colony responds quickly and effectively to their environment. What is mind boggling is that the ants do this with a minimal amount of meetings and virtually no coffee – other than the occasional Starbucks spilled on the old anthill. So the question becomes: What makes swarms of ants and schools of mackerel successful? In my opinion there are five traits. These qualities also serve high performing business units quite nicely as well:

The action element of creating selflessness is to lavishly reward team-oriented behavior that delivers results. While individual achievement is still rewarded, the lavish element associated with team thinking will eventually become more sought after and, over time, create a positive shift in your team's culture.

1. **Empowerment**. Each individual in the swarm not only is empowered to make important decisions, but they feel empowered to make decisions without the fear of harsh recourse from their peers or leader. A great example of an empowered workforce is Ritz Carlton. Each employee is empowered to spend a certain amount of money per guest, if necessary, in order to ensure that their guest's stay is extraordinary.

2. **Cooperation**. As decisions are made, members of the swarm support the decision, as well as the decision-maker. Likewise, if a better decision presents itself, the swarm changes direction quickly, with no pushback from the original decision-maker.

3. **Coordination**. The group focuses on the major task at hand and strives to move in the same direction.

4. **Selflessness**. The swarm acts as one large unit. While each individual member possesses an identity, the mantra of "the whole being greater than the sum of its parts" courses through their collective veins. In other words, team accomplishment, not individual glory, is the most satisfying end. Many leaders ask me, "So just how is selflessness created in the workplace?" A great question. The easy answer is to make it a value of your corporate

culture – like agility. The action element of creating selflessness is to lavishly reward team-oriented behavior that delivers results. While individual achievement is still rewarded, the lavish element associated with team thinking will eventually become more sought after and, over time, create a positive shift in your team's culture.

5. **Results-Driven**. It is clearly understood by the swarm that positive results are paramount. In the swarm's case results are often a matter of life and death.

So what happens when the swarm puts these five qualities together? More often than not, they achieve success. Can we achieve great success by emulating nature? When it comes to exhibiting the above five qualities the answer is a resounding "you betcha!"

## Bottom Line

Create an empowering work environment that values cooperation, selflessness, and results. Then, go out there and swarm – intelligently.

# Part V

# Execution, Coaching, and Celebration

*At this point your team is armed with a proper collaborative structure, a vision that is widely embraced, heightened levels of communication and clearly understood expectations. It is now time to execute. The execution process is typically accompanied by a fair amount of coaching and celebrating. Together they culminate in solid results. Together, they lead to victory!*

# Chapter 20

# Execution

"What do think about your team's execution?"
"I think it's a good idea."

—An exchange between a reporter and Tampa Bay Buccaneers coach John McKay during his team's 26 game losing streak.

AS leaders, we focus a great deal on communication and management. But what are we truly seeking? Most of the leaders and teams I work with are seeking consistent, world-class execution, and why not? After all, the reputation and future profit of your business basically boil down to how well your team executes their mission.

But just what is execution? A definition that I have heard and like is, "the delivery of our promises." So just how do we, as leaders, ensure world-class execution? It starts with a series of reflective questions that leaders can ask themselves:

1. **Does my team have the right people onboard and the wrong people off board?** Keeping the wrong people on your team for too long can turn out to be a colossal mistake. Underachievers drain

the energy and spirit out of an otherwise healthy organization. The right people however, keep positive energy flowing and tasks being done correctly.

2. **Have I created and am I maintaining an environment that is agile?** Recall from chapter two that agility, not flexibility is specifically referenced and valued. Flexibility connotes a reaction, while agility infers that team members are anticipatory. The difference between being anticipatory and adjusting prior to hazards arising, versus reacting when hazards strike, can be the difference between achieving world-class results or simply palatable results. Seek to build an agility mindset – the results will amaze you.

3. **Have I set clear goals and priorities?** By effectively using working agreements and other communication tools, individual expectations, as well as group achievement should be clearly understood.

4. **Have I created and am I effectively using a dashboard that highlights the top result-drivers for my team?** By carefully measuring as many key results as possible, leaders will effectively enhance the proper focus of their team members.

5. **Are my high achievers being appropriately rewarded?** The key word here is appropriately. Make certain that high achievers are being rewarded in a manner that they value. How is this attained? By asking each team member what moves them and how they like to be rewarded. If anyone responds by saying "nothing," they are fibbing – push the issue, and their envelope. Everyone likes to be stroked. It is your job to find out just what buttons need to be pushed to passionately move your people.

6. **Am I driving stimulating training initiatives?** If you have team members who are younger than the baby boomer generation,

I strongly recommend having a formal training curriculum laid out that they can grasp and follow. Many organizations have experienced younger people in the workforce who appear to be constantly preparing for their next job. By continually training younger workers and helping them grow their skills, younger team members can be retained much longer than they would otherwise.

7. **Am I taking personal responsibility for my team delivering outstanding results?** Courageous leaders have the guts to bet their reputation on their team's performance. If you can answer "yes" to the previous six questions, I guarantee that you lead a team on which you can bet the farm.

## Bottom Line

World-class execution is spawned by creating a winning atmosphere, populating it with the right people, challenging them to continually grow, and rewarding the heck out of achievement along the way.

## Chapter 21

# Planning for Action

IN chapter six we addressed the concept of "your actions speak so loudly, I cannot hear a word you say." This phrase rings true on many levels. After all, no organization will succeed without action. Therefore, the time has come to address action planning. Action plans are an effective communication tool for identifying, tracking, and driving execution and superior results.

In this instance, action planning means creating a set of deliverables that will be accomplished by specific team members within a specified period of time. A plan of action can be created for a given month, quarter, year, or even longer. In addition, an executable plan of action is a living document that thirsts to be updated on a monthly or quarterly basis.

An executable plan of action is a living document that thirsts to be updated on a monthly or quarterly basis.

There are six steps to the action planning process:

1. **List tasks – be specific**. The key here is to catalog all possible tasks that make sense to pursue. Do not get caught up with trying to

rate or prioritize the tasks at this point. Simply use brainstorming in order to create an atmosphere that lets ideas flow.

One of the pragmatic outcomes that results from effective action planning is the realization that not all of your team's intended actions can be accomplished.

2. **Point person**. For each task, identify who will be responsible for its completion. If a task is assigned to a group, choose a point person for the group who will have ultimate accountability for the task's completion.

3. **Due date**. Set a time specific date by which the task is to be accomplished. For example, rather than writing "first quarter of year," say "complete by 3/15/__." It is important that the point person commits to the date, as opposed to having the date assigned to them.

4. **Measure**. If it is possible to measure the successful outcome of the task, state specifically how the task will be evaluated. For example, if it is a sales task, track what was sold, as well as its impact on the bottom line.

At this point, the headings of a plan of action should mirror the template shown below.

| Task | Who Owns It | Due Date | Measurability |
|---|---|---|---|
| | | | |
| | | | |

5. **Refine**. The next step of the action planning process is to reduce the number of items appearing on the list by crossing off tasks that are unattainable or are of lesser importance. One of the

pragmatic outcomes that results from effective action planning is the realization that not all of your team's intended actions can be accomplished. This is a good thing. It allows leaders and teams to pare items that, while valid, do not carry enough cache to be considered a top priority.

6. **Prioritize**. While action plans are usually organized by due date, it is more important to segment the report by whatever delineation makes sense for your team (i.e., by bottom line impact, customer need, department goal, ease of completion, etc.). When an action plan is created and managed correctly, it serves as a focusing tool that assists teams in maintaining laser-like vision on items that are truly critical. The action plan then becomes a wonderful tool that leaders can use to maintain a focus on priorities. In this regard, the next chapter will expand our look at priority management.

When an action plan is created and managed correctly, it serves as a focusing tool that assists teams in maintaining laser-like vision on items that are truly critical.

## Bottom Line

Create an exhaustive list of meaningful actions and pare them down to the most essential and pragmatic items. Then, focus on action and lead your team to world-class execution.

CHAPTER 22

# Priority Management

SUSAN works for a fast-paced, quality-oriented organization. Changes in strategy and procedure are commonplace. She is a terrific professional: hard-working, intelligent, and articulate. She cares about the eight people she leads, and is committed to providing solid results for her department and the overall organization. There is one problem, however. Susan often leads her team in one direction, while the organization is moving in a slightly different direction. This befuddles Susan to no end. Especially since she is a good listener and places proper focus on goals. So what is going on here? What is creating a disconnect between the excellence that Susan seeks and the average performance that she and her team deliver?

The answer lies in the fact that there is substantial lag-time between the declaration of changes in organizational priorities and those changes being communicated to Susan. This dynamic is unfortunately commonplace. For example, Susan's organization began the year with five key initiatives or outcomes in focus. By the end of the first quarter, due to changes in the marketplace (i.e., competition, regulation, opportunity, etc.), five new initiatives or outcomes gained priority. As a result, Susan is fervently leading her team with yesterday's playbook.

Keep in mind that Susan's boss is not intentionally keeping her in the dark. He is simply overwhelmed with his own tasks, goals, and organizational changes. What Susan, and more importantly, her boss need is a tool to manage shifting organizational priorities. They need a "priority communication tool."

A Priority Communication Tool (PCT) is a model that enables leaders to communicate top organizational priorities in an effective way and on a regular basis. Often times, a company's top priorities are the same from month-to-month. Other times, however, particularly during periods of rapid change, priorities can frequently shift. Even though top leaders believe they have effectively communicated new priorities, a PCT ensures that a clear message regarding the changes has been delivered. It should be noted that the number of items listed on the PCT may vary from 5 to 25, or more. What is important is that mission critical items are listed, and items that are no longer a top priority are deleted. In a moment a sample PCT will be presented. First, let's examine some types of PCTs.

A Priority Communication Tool (PCT) is a model that enables leaders to communicate top organizational priorities in an effective way and on a regular basis.

## Types of Priority Models

Depending upon the size and structure of your organization, it may make sense to create several PCTs. Some of the areas deserving of a PCT include the following:

- Organization – in order to communicate broad corporate initiatives
- Division – in order to couple corporate vision with division goals
- Region (geographic or market segment) – in order to embrace corporate initiatives with expected regional outcomes

- Department – to keep a focus on the organization, while accomplishing tasks
- Workgroup – to maintain a connection to a broader vision, while executing duties
- Product line – to embrace corporate initiatives and match product line accomplishments with them
- Job function – to maintain a corporate to team-member connection

## Sample Priority Communication Tool

A sample PCT is provided as a guide for your use and customization.

| Priority* | Level** | Comments |
|---|---|---|
| 1. Increase sales by 20% for the year | 1 | This continues to be the company's top priority. |
| 2. Implement new customer service strategy | 1 | Effective next quarter this is a number 1 priority. |
| 3. Discontinue old customer service model | 5 | At the end of this quarter we abandon this strategy. |
| 4. HR streamline initiative | 2 | This will be ongoing for the remainder of the year. |
| 5. Team member development initiative | 2 | This is ongoing via a series of podcasts and online streaming video training. |

* A priority may be a task, a corporate initiative, a change in philosophy, etc.
** The level may be shown as a number or shown by color. The following guide is offered for your consideration.

| | |
|---|---|
| Mission Critical: | 1 or green |
| Important: | 2 or blue |
| On Hold: | 3 or yellow |
| Low: | 4 or orange |
| Deleted: | 5 or red |

## Frequency of Communication

Some of the determining factors regarding the frequency of distributing the Priority Communication Tool are:

- The amount of change your organization is experiencing or anticipating
- Your team's needs
- Your team's normal communication channels and frequency of communication

## Means of Communication

It is up to the leader to decide the best method to communicate the model:

- Email
- Verbal (at meetings)
- Memo (paper or electronic)
- As part of a formal report
- All of the above

Let us return to the saga of Susan and her boss for a moment. A model similar to the one described above was shared with Susan's boss. He embraced it. After all, he was frustrated too and was delighted to receive a tool that could enhance communication and understanding. The timeframe he chose for distribution was weekly. Soon Susan and her team were receiving updates that kept their heads spinning. As a result, Susan's department engaged in strategic brainstorming and action planning. They reorganized the structure and flow of information within their department in order to better fit with the direction of the organization. At the end of the day, Susan and her team felt a part of something meaningful, as opposed to sitting on the outside of chaos, looking in.

## Bottom Line

If you desire a nimble organization filled with agile team members, create crystal clarity regarding targeted priorities. Restate your team's top priorities on a regular basis. The reinforcement will keep corporate and individual priorities in focus with all team members.

# Chapter 23

# Put Me In Coach

"Oh, put me in, Coach - I'm ready to play today"

—John Fogerty

ALL athletes and most business people believe they are ready for prime time. They want to get in the game and show their stuff. Competitive zeal is admirable. Most leaders thirst for a team of go-getters who are anxious to achieve. Let's step back for a moment, however, and reflect on the leader as a coach. The coaching world contains a different flavor of leadership. Coaching calls for the following interesting mix of qualities:

1. The ability to select the right players
2. Motivation and retention of team members
3. Tools and techniques to help team members grow as professionals
4. The grit to frequently share feedback and continually challenge people to achieve

We begin examining the leader as a coach by delving into the topic of choosing the right players.

## Select the Right Players

A foundational skill a coach should possess is the ability to recruit and land the right players for his or her team. You can be the best coach in the world at teaching technical skills, but if your team is populated with mediocre talent, odds are good that mediocre results will follow. In addition, studies have shown that aligning the right team member with the right "job fit" can positively impact work performance by more than 25%.[9] As such, I recommend the following steps for attracting and selecting the best band of prime time players:

1. **Be a scout**. In other words, constantly be on the lookout for talent. Think about it this way, every week we meet someone who impresses us with their level of service, subject knowledge, or incredible professionalism. Ponder if these people could fit into your business. Most will not, but a few may have potential. Regardless, the scouting activity in and of itself will help put you in a healthy mindset regarding the pursuit of talent.

2. **Communicate with colleagues**. A coach should frequently remind colleagues that they are hunting for talented people. Whether the colleagues are part of your organization does not matter. What does matter is that you clearly and frequently communicate your interest in discovering good talent.

3. **Interview mania.** Let's be honest, interviewing is a pain in the neck. Many leaders consider interviewing a waste of time. As a result their interviews tend to be infrequent, too short, and of shoddy quality. The ability to conduct an excellent interview, however, is paramount to selecting the right people for your team. As such, I strongly recommend becoming a student of interviewing. Seek to utilize interview templates and guides that assist with the flow and consistency of your interaction with

candidates. The results will be better hiring decisions and a reduction in employee turnover.

## Motivation & Retention

Most everyone enjoys positive attention. By offering meaningful coaching, leaders supply important attention to team members that provides at least five benefits.

1. **Bonding**. Effective coaching creates a bond between a leader and a team member. In my opinion, team members who feel a positive connection to a leader and their organization are better motivated to achieve standout results.

2. **Healthy culture**. Coaching sends a message that your organization values communication. This leads to the creation or reinforcement of communication and coaching as part of the organization's corporate culture.

3. **Powerful learning**. Coaching provides a reliable platform for team members to improve skills and learn new techniques. In addition, because coaching topics are tied directly to daily experiential activities and delivered in a one-on-one setting, the impact of the coaching process far exceeds results achieved by reading books or viewing instructional videos.

4. **Performance identifier**. Good coaches have their fingers on the pulse of each team member's performance. This provides a huge leadership advantage to professionals who embrace coaching. The process of coaching makes it abundantly clear who is performing and progressing and who is floundering. As a result, a retention wall can be built around your best performers, while early, corrective action can be taken with poor performers. Ultimately, positive results are increased, and your company's payroll investment is maximized.

5. **Retention**. The stimulation of positive coaching and professional growth typically results in team members who choose to remain with an organization longer than if coaching were absent. Thus, coaching is an effective retention tool.

## Growing People

The creation and sharing of a formal coaching plan is a crucial step in the development process.

The cornerstone of coaching is the ability to develop talent. It is not easy, but the best coaches I know embrace the following six philosophies:

1. **Coaching is constant**. Developing people is not an occasional or one-time event. Rather, informal coaching is an activity that powerful leaders engage in every day. If you want your team to consistently perform at a high level, make certain you observe team member behaviors and proactively coach on a daily basis.

4. **Ownership**. It is the coach's responsibility to drive formal development activities. While team members certainly have a huge stake, the learning process should be driven and monitored by the coach.

5. **Have a plan**. The creation and sharing of a formal coaching plan is a crucial step in the development process. It is a growth roadmap that serves as a compliment to the casual coaching that you offer each day. A coaching plan should contain an outline of the process, the results that are desired, a list of the team member's strengths, and a detail of the topics that will be covered over a specified timeframe. The rollout of each coaching plan, as well as the process itself, should be conducted on a one-on-one basis.

6. **Partnership**. Once a formal coaching plan has been discussed with a team member, it is important to seek their buy-in. You may ask them to demonstrate their commitment by signing the coaching plan. In addition, after each formal coaching session it should be agreed that the team member provide a one-page written summary of the session. The summary should contain a recap of the topic, feedback on the session's impact, and an evaluation of the overall value of the session. When team members create a written summary it further engages them and reinforces their commitment to professional growth.

When team members create a written summary it further engages them and reinforces their commitment to professional growth.

7. **Tailor**. While you may possess a particular coaching style, a good coach is often a chameleon. It may be necessary for you to adjust your coaching style so that it fits seamlessly with a team member's personality, skill level, experience, and potential. More than likely the members of your team have varied levels of the above traits. As such, their needs will call for you to adjust your approach in order to be the most effective coach for them.

8. **Time allocation**. It is a brutal reality, but a coach only has so much time to offer team members. As such, it is critical that coaches "force rank" team members from most valuable to least valuable in order to clearly understand who the high performers are, as well as who possesses high potential. By allocating the lion's share of your time to high-value categories you will be maximizing your team's potential results. Spending an unfair share of your time coaching underperformers is unfair to the people who are producing, and will ultimately stunt your team's results. Picture a basketball game. Who does the coach talk with most during the game, the people on the bench or the people scoring the points?

Picture a basketball game. Who does the coach talk with most during the game, the people on the bench or the people scoring the points?

## Communication & Feedback

The hallmark of an effective coach is their ability to deliver feedback that sticks. It is an *art* to position team members so that they are receptive to feedback. In addition, it takes discipline, organization, and solid observation skills to be able to offer feedback on a regular basis. As we learned in Feedback Frenzy way back in chapter five, there are several key actions to delivering effective feedback. From a coaching perspective, here are six steps to consider.

1. **Ask and tell**. The first step in delivering feedback is to ask team members what they expect to receive. Do they prefer face-to-face coaching sessions, teleconferences, emails, summary reports or all of the above? In addition, if you have a preferred style or method, share your thoughts with the people you coach. Let them know what to expect from you, and tell them what kind of behavior and results you expect.

2. **Catch people doing something right!**[10] It is our strengths that make us successful. As such, be observant of other's strengths, best practices, and achievements. Once positive behaviors or outcomes have been observed, promptly give the team member positive reinforcement.

3. **Mind the math**. My experience has shown that people tend to respond to feedback that is slanted to the positive. A ratio to keep in mind is three pieces of positive feedback to every one piece of constructive feedback. Now, if someone has totally screwed up, it certainly is appropriate to delve more heavily into the constructive. Under normal circumstances, however, a 3:1 ratio (positive to constructive) works nicely. Focusing on a 3:1 ratio also places emphasis on identifying several specific positives, while paring down potentially negative comments to only the most necessary.

4. **Tone & Body Language**. It is critical that the tone of voice and body language that you use while coaching is consistent with the message that you are delivering. Good eye contact, a confident tone, and open body language, coupled with the appropriate words and timing can add up to a powerful coaching lesson that deeply resonates with a team member.

5. **Be specific**. General statements such as "good job" or "please do better next time" have minimal impact. Yes, they let people know that you are aware of their performance, but it does not give them something specific to repeat or correct. As such, seek to highlight specific behaviors that team members exhibit, as well as the specific results their actions achieve. If you deliver constructive feedback, make certain you describe the correct behavior, as well as the enhanced results you expect. Following are two examples: one of positive reinforcement and one of a constructive nature.

- **Positive Feedback**: You observe a team member deliver superior customer service. Rather than saying "Good job helping Mr. Smith," consider expanding your statement by saying: "Nice job assisting Mr. Smith. You used his name several times, clearly acknowledged his request, proactively offered a solution, and confirmed that you would follow up with him next week – bravo!"

- **Constructive Feedback**: You observe a team member deliver sub-par customer service. Avoid making a general statement such as: "That's not the way we do things around here, I expect better next time." Instead, be specific and in a professional (non-terse) tone, offer this: "You did a good job of using the Mr. Smith's name, as well as clearly summarizing his request. He seemed taken aback, however, by the harsh tone of voice you used and your lack of quality control – you did not offer to follow up with him. Please pay better attention to using a professional tone. Also, by delivering thorough follow up, you will increase the chance that the customer will be happy and place future orders with us." Note: as soon as you observe the team member exhibit correct behavior, promptly share specific, positive feedback with them.

6. **Raise the bar.** High performing professionals enjoy being challenged. Do not hesitate to request that team members perform at a higher level. While doing so, communicate opportunities for advancement and monetary rewards associated with overachieving. Consider asking the people you coach to seek to be incrementally better today than they were yesterday. Building a mindset of continuous, incremental improvement can lead to a culture that is focused on quality and performance.

## Bottom Line

Effective coaching results in the following:

1. Team members with stronger skills and abilities
2. Enhanced rapport with team members
3. A healthy corporate culture
4. Better retention of key team members
5. Increased quality and productivity

## Chapter 24

# Celebrate

"Celebrate, celebrate, dance to the music!"

—Three Dog Night

NOTHING ushers in a final chapter quite like a set of cheesy pop music lyrics. Back when I was a pup I actually listened to Three Dog Night's music – ah, but I digress.

One of the things I really like about the above quote is the word "celebrate." It is an uplifting and fun activity that is worthy of your focus and energy.

When we observe athletic successes such as a football team playing in a super bowl or the U.S. National Women's Soccer team competing, what do we see? One of the prevalent visuals is grown people doing all sorts of smiling and hand slapping each time something good happens. We see blatant celebration. Why do these people, these teams, celebrate? The answer is: to share recognition, pump each other up, and build positive momentum. Sports teams desire many of the same qualities that leaders want from their people in the workplace – communication, collaboration, teamwork – results! So ask yourself these questions:

- What kind of celebrating am I leading in my office, business, or workplace?
- Do my people *recognize* the efforts as celebrating?
- Does our celebrating build morale and lift people to continuously new heights?

Here are three tips regarding celebration:

1. Ask your people how they want to celebrate.
2. Find out how your team members want to be recognized for the outstanding work they do every day.
3. Dare to double your team's current level of celebrating. You can do it – you won't be disappointed.

## Bottom Line

Celebrating lifts the human spirit and accentuates positive momentum. You can rarely go wrong with celebration. After all, as an effective leader graced with a team brimming with accomplishments, you will have a great deal to celebrate!

# Afterword

THERE is an ancient Zen story; in fact it is my favorite one. It goes something like this:

> A Western reporter visits a Zen master in order to learn why he is so wise and at peace. The Zen master warmly greets his guest and invites him to sit down; he offers him tea. After saying "yes" to tea, the reporter begins to ask questions that are filled with pre-conceived notions. Without responding the Zen master fills the reporter's cup with tea. Soon the cup is overflowing and the confused reporter begins yelling: "Hey, hey, my cup is full." Calmly the Zen master replies: "Before we can talk, you must first empty your cup."[11]

Hmmm, so the question that might be burning in your mind right now is "why the heck is he sharing this little tea-time tale with me?" The answer is as follows:

The reporter's mind was filled with all sorts of pre-conceived notions (head trash) that were preventing him from learning and growing. Shifting gears: we work with talented, smart people every day. It's motivating and inspiring really. However, all too often the talented people we connect with have placed boundaries on themselves. Now, in their defense they may believe that their company, or society, or time constraints, or something else has set these boundaries. More often than not, however, my experience has shown that we set our own boundaries. Pogo once said: "We have met the enemy and it is us," and you know, it's kind of true.

So at the close of this book I want to share with you the biggest tip I can give anyone – no lie – it is the biggest. Here it is: open your mind to your *real* potential! Seek to free yourself of head trash and constraints that aren't really constrictive in the first place. Oh, and stop worrying – it just tires us out. Instead focus on being positive. Visualize your potential. Think of your potential as a possession - something priceless, yet readily attainable. Figure out a way to measure your progress as you push your envelope. Remember you can only manage what you can measure. The process then becomes a matter of implementation, which counter-intuitively is the easiest part of improved results.

## Bottom Line

Help set people free from their head trash. Challenge yourself and your team to take their strengths to a higher level and to do a few key things differently in order to enhance their performance. Good luck and be well!

# Notes

1. Corporate Leadership Council® study, *Managing for High Performance and Retention*, 2006, page 14.
2. Learning and Teaching Scotland, *The Learning Brain*, 2007, page 2.
3. Corporate Leadership Council® study, *Managing for High Performance and Retention*, 2006, page 11.
4. Marcus Buckingham & Donald O. Clifton, *Now, Discover Your Strengths*, (The Free Press 2001) p. 121.
5. Albert Mehrabian, *Silent Messages*, Wadsworth Publishing Company, 1971.
6. San Jose State University report on *Dale's Cone of Experience*, 2004, page 2.
7. Corporate Leadership Council® study, *Managing for High Performance and Retention*, 2006, page 4.
8. Jim Collins, *Good to Great*, (Harper Business 2001) p. 92.
9. Corporate Leadership Council® study, *Managing for High Performance and Retention*, 2006, page 14.
10. Kenneth Blanchard and Spencer Johnson, *The One Minute Manager*, William Morrow and Company, Inc.
11. Paul Reps and Nyogen Senzaki, *Zen Flesh Zen Bones*, (Tuttle Publishing 1998) p. 19.

# Index

# About DVD Consulting

## Belief Statement

WE believe in continually striving for excellence; in focusing on enhanced productivity; and in relentlessly pursuing wise and positive action. Individuals and organizations that embrace these high standards typically experience increased revenues, controlled expenses, and maximized net income. High standards also result in satisfied customers and team members that believe in and hold a strong connection to the leaders and the organization.

These thoughts guide us; these thoughts are our commitment.

## Programs and Services

Keynotes, half and full day programs, coaching, and consulting are all available to help you and your team enhance skills and performance. Our most popular offerings are listed below.

**Leadership Simplified.** This program or keynote highlights the concepts presented in the book, and customizes them to your organization.

**Sales Simplified.** "Nothing happens until someone sells something" is an age-old mantra for businesses around the world. Yet as the world rapidly changes, many organizations are selling the same way they did many years ago. *Sales Simplified* takes you and your team through a process whereby they communicate smarter, break bad habits, learn good habits, and sell more as a result.

**Productivity Simplified.** Fun and productive teambuilding and skill building sessions help grow professionals in a manner that encourages and promotes team accomplishment.

**Consulting.** Is your business facing hurdles? Perhaps there are opportunities that need to be fleshed out? Are you challenged with issues involving people and processes; sales and marketing; growth or divestiture? Consulting can provide a path that leads to smart solutions!

**Coaching.** Coaching topics are available for leaders and for the valued team members they lead.

- ***Leading with Passion.*** Learn how to build on strengths and identify new areas of potential. You will be provided with new leadership tools that will help you lead your team and maximize their productivity.

- ***Effective Communication.*** Enhance your communication skills with sniques that will help your team members hear what you say, and retain what is important.

- ***Building A Powerful Day.*** The difference between excellent performance and mediocre performance often lies in how effectively time has been used. Personalized effectiveness coaching will teach you systems and provide specialized tools that will maximize the value of every hour.

- ***Coaching & Developing Team Members.*** Studies have shown that consistent development of staff members reduces employee turnover and leads to greater levels of employee satisfaction. Learn how to continually develop high-performing and high-potential team members in a powerful and meaningful manner.

**To learn how Doug Van Dyke will help you energize your leadership abilities call 1.941.776.1121 or visit www.dvdconsulting.com.**

# About The Author

DOUG VAN DYKE is a speaker, training expert, consultant, and executive coach who has worked with organizations across the country for over 25 years. He has coached individuals and helped them realize more of their potential. Doug has also led hundreds of seminars that have enabled groups of professionals to communicate more effectively, lead with passion, embrace change, increase the profitability of their organizations, and smile as they choose to have more fun at the game of work.

Doug's repeat client list includes: Humana, Nielsen Media Research, Sysco Foods, Bealls Department Stores, The University of South Florida, Assurant Employee Benefits, Lifepath Hospice, Revolution Money, and The Melting Pot Restaurants.

# Notes

# Notes

# Notes

# Notes